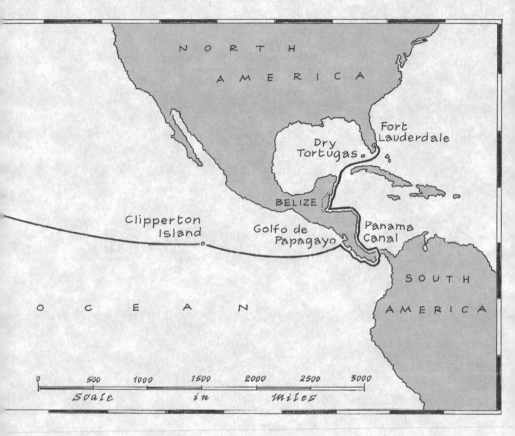

N O R T H

A M E R I C A

Dry
Tortugas.

Fort
Lauderdale

BELIZE

Clipperton
Island

Golfo de
Papagayo

Panama
Canal

S O U T H

A M E R I C A

O C E A N

| 0 | 500 | 1000 | 1500 | 2000 | 2500 | 3000 |

Scale   in   Miles

DARK
WIND

DARK
WIND

***

A Survivor's Tale
of Love and Loss

GORDON
CHAPLIN

ATLANTIC MONTHLY PRESS

NEW YORK

Published simultaneously in Canada
Printed in the United States of America

Endpaper chart copyright © 1997 Crown Publishers. Published at Taunton September 3, 1993 under the superintendence of Admiral J. A. L. Myres, C. B., FRICS, Hydrographer of the Navy. This chart includes copyright material published with the permission of the hydrographic offices of other nations.

The location of one incident has been changed to protect the privacy of individuals.
It is the author's intention that the net proceeds from the sales of this book will be used for the benefit of Susan Atkinson's daughters, Ashley and Page.

FIRST EDITION

Library of Congress Cataloging-in-Publication Data
Chaplin, Gordon.
Dark wind / Gordon Chaplin.
p. cm.
ISBN 0-87113-743-7
1. Pacific Coast (Central America)—Description and travel.
2. Hurricanes—Central America—Pacific Coast. 3. Chaplin, Gordon—Journeys—Central America—Pacific Coast. I. Title.
F1433.2.C45 1999
917.28'09636—dc21   98-49509
                                      CIP

DESIGN BY LAURA HAMMOND HOUGH

Atlantic Monthly Press
841 Broadway
New York, NY 10003

99 00 01 02   10 9 8 7 6 5 4 3 2 1

Contents

TO ASHLEY
AND PAGE

"Throughout the whole absurd life I'd lived, a dark wind had been rising toward me from somewhere deep in my future."

—*The Stranger*, Albert Camus

Gordon my love —
Isn't this card wonderfully
symbolic —

Susan

That Evening Sun

S unset. The air still smelling of rain after a thunder-storm, but clearing in a light, cool northwest breeze. New York's Hebron hills around me looking washed and clean. Thick, textured clouds slowly breaking up into light-shot crevasses and peaks, gold moving toward neon moving toward magenta: the promise of a fine night. At sea, it would have been perfect—easy sailing ahead, watching the stars.

How would she look? Rapt. No one could look more rapt at sunset. What would she say? Probably nothing; we never talked much while we watched the sun go down.

I pour her glass full of champagne and put it on top of a big round hay bale. The bale is almost at the top of the hill, which is the highest point for maybe twenty miles around—one of her favorite places. To the west, the purpling Adirondacks across the Hudson Valley where the sun is setting. To the east, the Taconic range of Vermont fading into gray. Our yellow house at the foot of the hill, hidden by green woods. Bubbles rising in the champagne, catching the changing light.

Earlier that day a letter had arrived:

I understand that everything that happened did so because it was part of a whole pattern of your lives, a pattern of courage and foolishness, daring plans and flawed judgment.

Is it true? Did the pattern of our lives lead inexorably to disaster? And, if so, why have I been left to stand alone on the top of a hill in upstate New York while the sun goes down another time, and another, and I watch summer give way to fall, fall to winter, and the twentieth century give way to the twenty-first?

I am beginning to realize that I have to write our story. By the time I finish, maybe I'll understand it.

I step back and hoist my glass. At this point she'd raise one eyebrow and say, "Here's *looking* at you," our old sappy toast, the one we gave each other every sunset for thirteen years, and I'd pull down my upper lip like Bogart and answer, "Here's looking at *you*." But something else comes out. I'm shocked to hear it, to have it hanging in the air between us.

"Susan, is it all right? Can you forgive me?"

OUR LUXURY

Into the Blue

November 1989. We started our voyage with that same toast, sitting side by side in the cockpit as the sun went down into the stately purple wave tops, with Fort Jefferson in the Dry Tortugas a vanishing red dot in our wake and 290 miles of flying fish, sargasso weed, and blood-warm Gulf Stream ahead of us. We were bound for the Mosquito Coast of Central America, with a 20-knot easterly breeze on the port quarter and all sails set and drawing.

"Will you just give me a little pinch?" Susan asked, after the toast. "Not *too* hard."

I had my arm around her. I reached my hand up and pinched her nose, something I loved to do because her nose was long, thin, and sensitive.

"Perfect. Dow I doe id's really habbenig."

I let go of her nose and rested my hand on her shoulder while she took hold of a finger. I wanted to tell her that the main reason it was happening was because of her, but instead I said, "Maybe it isn't. Maybe we're just in the same fantasy."

"That's okay," she said softly. "But if it's yours, you have to promise me something, all right?"

"Sure," I said proudly. "Anything you want."

"No surprises. Anything can happen, but you have to tell me about it first."

I inherited the fantasy from my father, who was on his way from England to the South Pacific in a small sailboat when he met my mother and came ashore to live out his days comfortably in Philadelphia. I'd always thought he had taught me boating so I could continue the voyage, and continuing it now, among other things, seemed a perfect way to atone for my various shortcomings as a son.

Susan entered the fantasy for the first time in the midsixties. She was married to my college roommate, Bill. I was married to my college sweetheart, Holly. Bill and I were working as reporters on a little newspaper outside Boston, and for a week's vacation the four of us chartered a sailboat in Maine.

For the last two years I'd known Susan first as Bill's witty, slightly racy girlfriend and then as his hardworking no-nonsense wife. During Bill's community activism phase in Roxbury, she supported them both on her nurse's salary from Massachusetts General Hospital. And under the pressure she'd developed a famously short fuse.

Holly had grown up sailing with her father and was the most cautious aboard. Bill was the best blusterer. I was Captain Horatio Hornblower; my job was to inject risk and drama into what otherwise might have been a pretty humdrum sail.

On the last day of the cruise we set out from Pulpit Harbor on the island of North Haven across Penobscot Bay back to Camden. A mile or so out, the black line squall bearing down on us from the west became impossible to ignore. Holly wanted to return to harbor before it struck, I wanted to continue out and get some sea room. Bill swallowed hard and sided with Holly.

We all looked at Susan. She had a strong jaw as well as a distinguished nose. Her eyes were deep set, steady and gray. Her lips were thin and straight, and her waist-length dark-blond hair was in a tight bun. She looked very Bostonian. "I agree with Gordon," she said to Holly and Bill, and I felt my chest expand. "We're not going to make it back before that hits. We should get farther out."

"You don't know what you're talking about, Susan," Bill said.

"Well, then I'll let you experts handle it." She got up and went below.

The squall didn't look that bad: a narrow band of inky clouds followed by lightening sky and even a patch or two of blue in the distance. "Yeah," I said. "You experts take her in." And I went below too.

We sat on opposite settees in the small snug cabin and looked at each other shyly. I tried a smile; she returned it. Our knees touched, and I noticed that her eyes—which could be very wintry—were soft and unfocused, and their pupils enlarged. Her mouth was open a little in concentration or breathlessness; she raised her hand absently to straighten the hair at the back of her head, showing me her palm.

Through the open hatch we could hear Bill and Holly making frantic preparations on deck. And we watched each other with a prickle of something that seemed more important than simply agreeing you don't run from a little bad weather. More important even than the secret acknowledgment that we'd both probably enjoy the rush.

The storm hit long before we made it back to harbor. Now, framed by the hatch, our two spouses seemed like actors in a badly staged movie from the thirties: sheets of fake-looking rain, wind tearing the words from their lips, flapping sails. We looked at each other again and burst into perfectly synchronized laughter. By the time we emerged from the cabin (a strand of her hair blowing loose across my eyes) we were laughing so hard we were almost no help at all.

* * *

Twelve years came and went. We each had two daughters. Along different routes, Bill and I had moved from the small newspaper outside Boston to the *Washington Post*. I'd helped him get the first job; he helped me get the last. Bill and Susan's marriage had fallen apart; Holly and I were on shaky ground. This was the late seventies.

It swept in and carried us away like an unavoidable force of nature: an illicit, dangerous romance of shared secrets and wild exuberance that seemed to pick up where we'd left off in the cabin of the little boat. And as I witnessed the wreckage of my family I tried to take some comfort from its apparent inevitability.

Within six months I'd left my wife and daughters in Key West, Florida, where I was on a leave of absence to work on a novel, and was sailing north to join Susan on a twenty-eight-foot wooden cutter I'd virtually been given by a man whose own marriage was on the rocks. I took only my clothes and papers and the indelible memory of how my older daughter's arms felt around my neck, and how her tears felt on my cheek, and the opaqueness of my younger daughter's eyes as I assured them that I'd be seeing them very soon. That in a way we'd see more of each other now than before, that what we were doing was extending the family like the Brady Bunch, not truncating it. That I wasn't abandoning them to run off with another woman—the mother of their childhood friends Ashley and Page.

Susan joined me whenever she could get time off from her job as a nurse-practitioner in Washington: days snatched with improbable excuses for exalted reunions and wrenching farewells in remote anchorages all along the Eastern seaboard. Summer was beginning, and the big hatch over the low forward berth where we slept was always open so we could see the stars.

Eventually, we found ourselves in New York harbor, en route to Massachusetts, where I hoped to find a buyer who might appreciate the old wooden boat. Late afternoon, with big summer clouds rising over the towers of Wall Street, the anchored freighters, and—over near the marshes on the Jersey shore—the rococo spires of Ellis Island and the Statue of Liberty.

"The Big Apple," I proclaimed. Susan didn't answer: the Silent Treatment. She hadn't spoken to me since early morning, when I'd tried to laugh off a canceled invitation from my parents in Philadelphia. (They were afraid our adulterous status might shock the maid.)

My plan was to shoot through the East River on the incoming tide and anchor for the night in the lower reaches of Long Island Sound. It would be an exciting ride. The tide at Hell Gate reaches seven knots at full flood, which was about when we'd get there.

Deep into the harbor, with the island of Manhattan dividing the water of the Hudson on the left from the East River on the right like some huge ocean liner, the wind failed. Susan silently took the tiller while I sheeted in the limp sails and started the engine. The hollow sound of the exhaust seemed to echo off the monstrous glass buildings, now melting into gold from the setting sun. The water was smooth and brown, with detritus swirling in the eddies from the increasing current. A tug pulling a garbage barge toward us out of the mouth of the river was kicking up a mountainous chocolate bow wave but gaining almost no ground against the landscape.

After about fifteen minutes of running, with the Brooklyn Bridge, the Manhattan Bridge, and the Williamsburg Bridge arching high and beginning to blink with the first lights of cars, I noticed the temperature gauge was reading well over boiling.

I shut down the engine.

"What?"

"Damn thing's overheating." I swung down into the cabin and began to remove the housing.

"What do I do?" In the fading light, framed by the companionway, she looked the opposite of scared. The Silent Treatment was over, thanks to nautical emergency.

"Just keep her off the shoals." I spat on the bare cylinder head and watched it sizzle. "It's probably the impeller."

I set about unscrewing the impeller cover, with a flashlight necessary to see the last screws. After I pulled the impeller, I held it up proudly so she could see how the rubber blades were perished and broken off. "Shot," I said. "I'll just put in the spare and we'll be fine."

She nodded. I felt good: competent and in control. I looked in the parts box for the spare, but there wasn't one.

I climbed back out into the cockpit with the flashlight, which we'd need for reading the chart. The current had carried us under the Manhattan Bridge opposite the old Brooklyn Navy Yard, but the setting sun was still visible over a last little section of New Jersey. I told Susan there was no spare impeller and kept my eyes on the sun. We were drifting helplessly, with no steerage way at all. I was thinking of the tugs and barges, the shoals at the end of Roosevelt Island, and, scariest of all, the dark abandoned piers and rusty pilings along the Brooklyn shore.

"Well," she said. "I put a bottle of champagne on ice this morning. We still have time to open it before sunset."

All I could do was stare in admiration. It wasn't as if she didn't know the dangers; we both knew them, but the toast had been her idea. The pop of the cork echoed festively in the dark canyons. Her rapt face over the rim of my full glass was the same face I'd recognized twelve years earlier before the storm in Maine. Her left eyebrow cocked. "Here's looking at you."

No harm came to us. Twisting and turning in the eddies but always just avoiding the obstacles, we drifted into a little cove at the north end of Roosevelt Island (mast clearing the forty-foot-high bridge by inches) and dropped anchor. More toasts and dinner in the cockpit, staring back at strollers in the little park on what the chart designated as Hallett's Point, Astoria. We fell asleep to the swish of traffic on the Triboro Bridge and, reflected on the mast, the neon blink of the big Brooklyn Pepsi-Cola sign.

A surprise came later. My ex-wife bought the boat after it finally arrived in her home state of Massachusetts, where she'd returned from Key West. She claimed half ownership, so I only got half the asking price. She sailed the boat to Edgartown on Martha's Vineyard, hauled her, and never got around to launching her again.

Eight more years came and went before Susan and I were able to buy another. We'd landed in upstate New York, weren't getting any younger, and the time to go adventuring seemed now. The greater Mosquito Coast, unsavory, inaccessible, and politically unstable, stretched down the eastern shore of Central America from Belize through Guatemala, Honduras, and Nicaragua to Panama. It was the destination of our dreams.

We planned to sail it. I had a contract for a travel essay book and Susan hoped to gather material for a novel, her third since leaving nursing to write full-time. We had no doubts our books would be terrific, though one reviewer was to write about mine, "Chaplin strains for charm but at the same time seems barely able to behave himself."

Well, nobody's perfect.

Our four daughters—whose ages interlock seamlessly a year apart beginning with her older, Ashley, twenty-one at the time, to my older, Diana, then Page, and finally Julie—were all in college. Mine were in California, so only hers were present at our farewell dinner in New York City in late October 1989.

Ashley and I arrived early at the restaurant. She was a senior at Wellesley, unassailably equipped with the kind of blond coolness that seems to go with political conservatism. She liked me about as well as Diana liked Susan. The younger ones were easier about things.

Ashley hardly ever saw me alone, so this was her chance to give me the third degree. She ordered Perrier and lime; I ordered a martini. We carefully went over the strengths and weaknesses of the new boat, the kind of weather we might encounter, our proposed itinerary, and how our responsibilities would be divided.

"Ashley," I said finally, "remember the *Christiana*?" The *Christiana* was a thirty-seven-foot Alden Challenger yawl our two families used to deliver places for her owner when the girls were young. "The *Sea Wand*? The *Ho Won*? Haven't we always done all right?"

"This is different," she said. "Nicaragua isn't exactly Maine."

"We sailed to Cuba twice. And the Bahamas. They're not exactly a piece of cake either."

"Plus you and Mom are going to be *by yourselves.*"

"Did you know," I said, "that at the age of fourteen I won the Pew Seamanship Trophy of the Bar Harbor Yacht Club?"

She just stared at me.

"And then"—I finished my martini and waved for the waiter—"at sixteen captained a Luders sixteen in the Northeast Harbor Cruise and won? Against forty other boats with seasoned skippers and crews twice my age?"

Her expression didn't change.

"I know the Third World pretty well too," I heard myself saying, "after the Peace Corps and two years in Southeast Asia as a war correspondent."

"You weren't in the Peace Corps."

"Well, I was in the training program. And Mexico. You ought to remember that." A low blow. At the beginning of our time together, Susan and I had taken her daughters to Mexico for what should have been a year. After six months, though, Ashley and Page had left—to live with their father in Rhode Island. It had been the low point in Susan's life with me.

Suddenly Ashley leaned forward and clasped my left hand as it lay on the table near the empty martini glass with both of hers. "You won't leave Mom alone on this trip, will you?"

She took me by surprise. After all, she was as fiercely self-reliant as her mother. "Well," I said defensively, "not unless I have to."

"What do you mean?"

"Things might come up, you know. Situations. That might make it unavoidable." I smiled and shrugged. "Separate adventures. Twice as much fun."

"You mean," she said slowly, letting go of my hand and straightening up, "you'd go off and leave her by herself?"

"Ashley. Your mother is perfectly capable of taking care of herself. You should know that better than anyone; she raised you to be like her."

She'd turned so pale I was afraid she was going to faint. "Over my dead body," she whispered.

"What?"

"Over my dead body you're going to go off and leave her alone. If you don't promise, I'll tie her to my bed so she stays with me."

It was an Ashley I'd never seen before. *"Promise,"* she whispered, as Susan and Page appeared in the door of the restaurant.

Susan's face was lit with pride, happiness, and a little nervousness, as she looked around trying to find us. Ashley whispered again and beat her fist gently on the table.

"All right." I looked at her quickly and then looked away again, like a child, waving to get Susan's attention. It was disturbing to think that Ashley might know something I didn't about Susan: what really lay behind her mother's adventurousness and determination. So, as I did with many troubling thoughts in those days, I shelved it—to be dusted off later, looking through her diaries in the small hours of a winter night.

Susan's daughters' going-away present to us was a rabbit's foot.

Night at sea. Twenty-three miles southwest of the Dry Tortugas, making 6.8 knots on a course of 255 degrees. The rabbit's foot hung from a hook in the wheelhouse just below the log, lit faintly by the dial's illumination and swinging with the boat's regular swoop and check. Without the engine, the only sounds were the gurgle and slap of waves

and the creak of the rigging. A three-quarters moon cre-
ated a mercurial highway to the east, the Whale Road. The
moonlit pearls of spray that made their way into the cockpit were the same temperature as the air.

"Ready for dinner?" Susan asked casually, as if we were
back at our place in upstate New York.

From the wheelhouse I could see down into the galley, see her cooking on the gimballed stove, leaning back
against a web belt attached to the counter, moving with
the boat as if she were part of it. I could smell fresh Gulf
shrimp, stir-fried vegetables, and egg noodles.

In front of me on the instrument panel the dials and
gauges glowed green, blue, red, white. I could hear the
light snore of the propeller turning as the water rushed past
at almost 7 knots. The autopilot, powered from the propeller shaft by a hydraulic system when the engine is off,
clicked the wooden wheel back and forth in small irregu-
lar arcs. Outside the wheelhouse, as I checked once again,
the running lights showed the sails full-bellied and drawing in the 20-knot breeze. The wake creamed white into
the black water, and the tip of the mast swung darkly through
the stars.

Excuses

Our new boat was not beautiful, not roomy, not fast. She was not airy or open or exquisitely crafted. She was seaworthy, Dutch-built, fanatically well equipped by her German owners, and looked like a North Sea fishing smack: large wheelhouse, stubby masts, heavy double-ended hull. She carried 350 gallons of diesel, giving her a range of 2,500 miles under power alone, and could do 7 knots under sail in a stiff, favorable breeze. At 36 feet, she was small enough for the two of us to handle easily, yet big enough to live aboard. The couple we bought her from had sailed her across the Atlantic and as far north as Labrador. They were in their sixties and passed her on to us, the next generation, with appropriate flourish.

The *Lord Jim,* she was called, and we hadn't changed the name because changing a boat's name is bad luck. We certainly didn't want to tempt the gods.

Susan had grown up with bad luck. Her father had been a suicidal manic-depressive, her twin brother would inherit the same condition. As the oldest of the remaining four children Susan had been the one her mother turned to in times of crisis. Instead of Harvard, like her brothers, she chose the nursing school at Massachusetts General Hospital, where she trained to cope with the same kind of situations that routinely occurred at home. With her quick reactions and cool head, she was soon running the emergency room.

Once upon a time, she was stopped in her old Ford Mustang at a red light in a bad part of Washington, D.C. Suddenly the passenger door opened and a smallish man climbed in. He warned her that if she screamed he'd kill her.

In the next breath, she hit the accelerator and wrenched the car into a U-turn. He hadn't yet closed the door, and in the middle of the turn she could see he was halfway out of the car, clutching for the door handle. Still swerving, she lifted her right foot from the accelerator, twisted her body, and kicked out at him. She caught him in the chest, and he was gone. Sweating and trembling, she drove for another mile or so, turned into a parking lot, rested her head on the steering wheel, closed her eyes, and gave way to an overpowering orgasm.

My own childhood had been well-fed and insulated, like a beaver's fatty tail. There was a home on Philadelphia's Main Line; summers in Bar Harbor; winters in Nassau. Good schools, well-groomed communities. No sharp edges, no pain. My parents were distant, not mentally ill. They gave my sister, Susie, and me everything they thought we needed.

I had nothing to overcome; Susan had too much. I had no real love; she had the wrong kind. Along opposite routes, we both arrived feeling like outsiders, strangers. And we both connected with crisis. To be solidly in the world, we needed to be on familiar terms with the chance of leaving it for good.

Once upon a time, I was on a deep dive over the dropoff north of Lyford Cay in Nassau. A friend came swimming frantically up to me, pulling his finger across his throat. He was out of air and knew nothing about SCUBA techniques except what I'd taught him the day before.

I passed him my mouthpiece. Whether he'd pass it back after a breath or two depended on factors I couldn't know, but I realized later that I was sure he would. Then I began to understand that I had never been surer of anything in my life. It was a moment of *satori*.

Would I have passed it to him if there had been doubt in my mind? I'll never know. But I know Susan would have. "You have to act fast when you make a decision," she used to say. "It might be the wrong one."

I loved her instinct that anything is better than standing still. I aspired to it. It's one of the reasons we were able to go.

Looking back, I see there was something eccentrically British about our departure—my father's influence? Americans tend to agonize over the moral issues of "taking off into the blue"—What about the kids? What about your responsibilities? What are you trying to prove? And (the most sanctimonious of all) how does it benefit mankind?—while the British have always recognized that some people are made to take off and have admired them for it.

Miles Smeeton, the British sailor (who was born the same year as my father), wrote the following in the epilogue of *Once Is Enough*, his account of being wrecked twice—and surviving—on successive attempts to round the Horn:

> Capes and seas, like mountains, "are there" to round
> and to cross; and adventure, even when not in search
> of knowledge and without scientific aim, is good for
> its own sake. Only when it involves other people un-
> wittingly or involuntarily in one's own distress is it bad.
> But even in this respect there may be another point of
> view, as Jim Byrne pointed out to us in Chile. "I think
> you ought to let people rescue you," he said. "It gives
> them a tremendous lift. The rescuer is always the hell
> of a chap, and the rescued gets slapped down. It's jolly
> decent of a chap to let himself be rescued."

In the end there are no excuses for what you do. An Apache fable that's always fascinated me begins with a scorpion sweet-talking an eagle into flying it across a river. Halfway there, the scorpion stings the eagle and they fall into the water. "Why did you sting me, brother?" the eagle asks. "Now we're both going to drown. Couldn't you see that?"

"Yes, I could see it," the scorpion replies. "But I had no choice. After all, I'm a scorpion."

Apparently, the eagle made the wrong decision. But maybe he had no choice either.

FUTILE THE WINDS

Peccadillo

The storms, hostile officials, reefs, sandbars, insects, breakdowns, and other obstacles that we ran afoul of on the Mosquito Coast just seemed to make us stronger. Like the squall in Penobscot Bay or the engine failure in the East River, each trial set us up better for the next.

There were no surprises. We'd review the dangers beforehand; then we'd make our move. So far, nothing had happened that we weren't prepared for.

Boat life agreed with us. The *Lord Jim* wasn't cramped; she was cozy. We loved to lie together in the forepeak late at night in a calm anchorage, listening to rain beating on the deck, draining into our tanks from our water catcher, knowing we were on our own and completely self-sufficient. During the day, moving around our vessel, we were constantly touching—brushing against each other on purpose and by accident. The contact was reassuring and necessary.

On board ship there's usually something that has to be done, and in the rare moments when there wasn't we'd read to each other or make love. Lovemaking was never better than when we were riding ten-foot waves hundreds of miles from land—Susan would be in a fantasy as usual, and if I asked her about it afterward she'd say, "If I told you, it would ruin it." Except once, when she admitted that I'd been an elephant seal.

If we'd been able to stay aboard the whole time, things would have been fine. They only get messy if you go ashore. . . . I guess it's been that way since the beginning of seafaring. Even the best seamen dread the vicissitudes of love.

The pier at the Fort George Hotel in Belize City was long and rickety, sticking out through brown shallow water into a large open bay with little protection. It wasn't the ideal place to tie up, but there was no choice. The main harbor was full of fishing smacks and commercial luggers, and the docks at night were reported to be dangerous. Most of the city's sewage, carried in open ditches, emptied into it too.

Seediness has always attracted me. "One of the last great fever ports of the world," I said proudly to Susan, as we sat in the cockpit after the immigration people had left. "'If the world has any ends, Belize is surely one of them.' Aldous Huxley wrote that."

Damp, fragrant heat wrapped around us like a rubber blanket. Susan sighed. "Have you ever wondered why you like these places so much?"

"Oh, come on, Susan. You like them too. Admit it."

"Not as much as you. You're a connoisseur." She wiped her damp forehead irritably with her forearm: we'd been sailing all night down the huge barrier reef ten miles offshore and were short on sleep. "Are we going to go ashore? Or are we just going to sit here and bake like yams?"

We secured the hatches and wheelhouse windows, locked the door, and turned on the alarm. I pulled the *Lord Jim* closer to the pier, held her while Susan clambered off, and jumped off myself. Still on our sea legs, we staggered down the long perspective toward the old deep-verandaed hotel, its white paint peeling. I was worrying about a Belizean girl named Consuela—Connie for short.

Next to the hotel was an overgrown park with a rusty wrought-iron kiosk in the center. A few loose-jointed black Belizeans were sitting and sleeping in the shade, although it was now late morning. Huge, white-eyed, blue-black boat-tailed grackles whistled insultingly from the poinciana and almond trees.

Wooden houses on pilings in the British Caribbean style of the hotel faced the park, and from one, almost hidden by a huge glowing purple bougainvillea, came the sound of someone playing a Chopin étude on a pretty good piano. Periodically, the person would repeat a section so we knew it wasn't a recording.

Susan's mouth opened, and the pupils of her eyes enlarged. "I can't believe it. My favorite piece." She looked at me, half scared, half transported (the same expression she had when the moon was full). "Oh, isn't it strange?"

"It's just Belize," I said, as comfortingly as I could. I'd been here before, three years earlier, on assignment for *Esquire* magazine to write a story on diving the atolls— among the few in the Atlantic—that lay outside the barrier reef. I'd gone out for a week aboard the dive boat *Gaviota* and fallen into a dalliance with the dive master, Connie. In the story I'd written, Connie's fling had been with a doctor from Philadelphia. And, of course, everyone's names had been changed.

At that point, Susan and I had been together for about five years. She'd read the piece carefully and then looked at me with a quizzical smile. "Nice writing. Especially about the romance. It wasn't you she had it with, was it? By any chance?"

"Of course not."

The smile was still there. "You wouldn't lie to me, would you?"

"Would *you* lie to *me*?"

"*Never.*"

"Well," I'd said, "I'm sorry if you think I'm so much less committed." I was quick to rationalize this lie with the overwhelming probability that I'd never see Connie again. And a shipboard dalliance is a shipboard dalliance.

Now, as we walked from the park across the low swing bridge over the fetid river that led into the harbor, through the smelly, exuberant, crowded market, past the scrolled and scalloped Victorian Colonial government building, I couldn't help being impressed at the poetic way chance had hung these rationalizations around my neck. Bypassing Belize to sail south to safer ground had been out of the question. The place was too important. At any moment Connie could appear. It seemed to be just a matter of time.

Everything I saw took on a special weight and poignancy. My senses were painfully alert, and I was aware that I was going to remember what I was seeing forever. This is the way to travel, I thought. As long as you can stand it.

Thanksgiving in Belize. We ate the local equivalent of turkey—Cow Foot Soup—in a one-room restaurant called the Joker. Heavy rain drummed on the tin roof, and the cable television system featured a Thanksgiving Day parade in Philadelphia, my hometown.

The thick spicy flavor sank deep into my taste buds. "Put some lead into your pencil, mahn." The waitress grinned at me, and I couldn't help blushing and glancing at Susan. I was sweating, too, the sharp acrid sweat of nervousness. I was sure she could smell it.

* * *

I'd smelled the same in her bedroom eight years earlier, after I'd heard her sobbing from the guest room across
the hall and knocked on her door. Her father had just died
in Florida of emphysema. I was in Washington on business. I sat down next to her on the bed and tried to say
something comforting. Then our hands touched and started
a caress as if they had a life of their own.

"Oh, God," she whispered. Exactly what happened
next is blurred, like the memory of your first roller-coaster
ride. But I remember worrying about the way I smelled—
sour as never before. And I remember my gratitude when
she whispered in my ear: "Don't worry, we'll have plenty
of time."

A couple of weeks later I'd returned to Key West and
we were corresponding —a letter a day, sometimes two—
for the next six months. She told me once that whenever
she was feeling blue she'd reread my letters. I'd hidden hers
up in the rafters of the carport in the Key West house, so I
couldn't do the same until years later when I recovered them.

This is like having a nervous breakdown. Visual
awareness I've never had. Walking along the sidewalk
and the geometrical squares looming toward me. At
the post office, hearing the sounds of the ropes hitting
the flagpole like halyards slapping against a mast.
Smelling the nervous sweat of a man in the supermar-
ket. Touching my own body and feeling both in my
fingertips and my breasts separately, distinct from each
other. Tasting the envelope gum as I mail your letters

to you. It's frightening and distracting and exhausting.
. . . I need to hear from you and know what your
thoughts are. If you're chickening out on this adventure, you must let me know.

And I'd written back:

No, I'm not scared of this adventure of ours. I
love it. It's unbelievable and wild. What I'm scared of
is *blowing it!*

All night, the Fort George Hotel pier was crowded
with Asians, fishing madly. The thump of stray lures on the
deck kept us awake. The Asians turned out to be illegal
Chinese immigrants who'd bought Belizean passports for
$20,000 a pop. They were waiting for transshipment to the
United States (another $15,000), and while they waited they
were catching their food.

I woke to a hot band of sunlight hitting my face
through the open hatch. Susan was already up. I lay there
still half in the dream I'd been having, at first just feeling
good about it, then beginning to itch with guilt. I'd been
out on a date with Barbra Streisand, and she'd been sur-
prisingly warm and easy to talk to. We'd had dinner and
gone for a long walk by the sea, just getting to know each
other.

In the galley, I could hear Susan making breakfast, a
series of familiar, domestic sounds. Still naked, I swung
down out of the forepeak, slid past the drop-leaf table in

the salon to the galley, where she was working (in a green tank top and khaki shorts, with her hair pinned up), and kissed her on the downy, sweet-smelling curve of her neck just below her hairline and above her shoulder.

She leaned away slightly. "You better put some clothes on. There's a lot of people around."

I had a quick cold shower. Toweling off, I looked out the head's porthole and saw the dive boat *Gaviota* tied up at the end of the pier, looking exactly as I remembered her. As if three years had never passed. Nobody was visible on board.

Susan suggested we carry our breakfast out into the cockpit, where there was a little fold-down table we often used in port, but I said I needed to transcribe my notes. We had a tight schedule, I reminded her. We were supposed to take a taxi ten miles out of town to the Belize Zoo. The lady zookeeper, whom I'd met while doing the diving story, was expecting us early.

"I don't think I'm going to go," Susan said. "I think I'll just spend the day on the boat."

I shrugged as casually as I could. "What's the problem?"

"We've been at sea for five days, in case you forgot. I'd like to just relax for a day. Plus my stomach feels a little queasy."

"Oh, come on. You love zoos, and Sharon is fantastic. The animals are like pets. There's one female mountain lion that's totally in love with her. You know why?"

"She feeds it Cow Foot Soup?"

"When it comes in heat she masturbates it. It's a common technique for animal trainers."

"*You* go," Susan said. "It sounds right up your alley."

"I can't go without you." I grinned. "Ashley ordered me not to leave you alone."

"Well, I'm ordering you to. So go. I won't tell her."

"Jesus." I shook my head. "You're in a foul mood this morning. What the hell's wrong?"

"I'm sick. Can't you understand that? I just need to be left alone."

I left in a snit. Also, with deep misgivings about what could happen while I was away. Maybe Susan didn't realize yet that the *Gaviota* was my old dive boat, but it was just a matter of time. Chances were, though, she already knew.

At the zoo, I simultaneously tried to hurry things up and draw them out. Sharon must have wondered what was going on, why I was so interested in waterfront gossip (she didn't know much), particularly about female dive masters (she was interested but hadn't heard of any), and why I couldn't stay for the evening meal at the jaguar house.

I knew one thing for sure: I had to get back to the boat in time for sunset. I made it with about half an hour to spare. Susan was sitting in the cockpit reading Eudora Welty's *One Writer's Beginnings*.

"So how was your day?"

"Oh"—she looked at me levelly—"I wrote and I read. And I walked and I talked."

"Really? Who with?"

"The dive master of the *Gaviota*, for one. A guy named John."

I nodded. "The girl you wrote about quit. Connie."

"Oh. What's she doing?"

"Why don't you ask her yourself?"

I stared at her. "Because I'm really not interested. Please give me a break."

I went down the companionway into the galley and dragged a bottle of cold Chardonnay from the icebox. I pulled the cork as hard as I could to make a resonating pop that I hoped would carry to the cockpit. I poured two full glasses and took them back up.

They chattered gently against each other.

By the time the glasses were empty, the sun was hovering in the tops of the tall mangrove trees at the western end of the bay. The afternoon breeze had dropped, and swallows were coursing the silky brown surface of the water for evening bugs.

"Want to go for a walk?" Susan asked.

"Sure," I said warily.

At the end of the pier I turned left, toward the overgrown little park, instead of right, along the *malecón* past a line of stately old houses on stilts.

"Let's go this way," she said. "These houses are worth seeing close up, don't you think?"

I shrugged in resignation. The houses, built around the turn of the century by well-to-do English planters who could afford the choice waterfront, *were* worth seeing. Their deep verandas were either open or closed off with wooden blinds. The large windows into the interiors each had a louvered shutter propped open by a stick. The gables were steep, with lacy Victorian gingerbread. The houses were all white, and the latticework that screened the space under them was green.

As we walked, Susan kept up a running commentary, but I was distracted by the house at the end. Ignoring what set it apart was harder and harder the closer we got. The low picket fence that had looked whitish from a distance was actually gray and rotting. The shrubs and grass that had looked lush were actually overgrown. The vague shapes through the broken latticework under the house resolved themselves into a limp black Zodiac inflatable on a rusty, flat-tired trailer, a couple of rusted steel SCUBA tanks, three or four outboard motors cannibalized for parts, and an ancient baby carriage full of old dive equipment.

Susan stopped on the *malecón* across the street from the house. The veranda blinds were closed, the shutters were closed. The steps leading up to the door to the veranda were gray as the picket fence. The house seemed to give off the smell of rotting flowers.

"What a crime," I heard myself say, after a while. "To let it go like that."

"Too seedy for you?" I could hear the tremor in her voice.

"It's not seedy. It's crossed the line."

"What is it, then?"

I stared for a while longer and shook my head. "I don't know. Sordid?"

She didn't say anything.

"Connie was raped right on those stairs," I said. "In her school uniform. They found the guy who did it passed out in the next yard. She grew up here, you know."

"Well, surprise," Susan said. "She's renting a room here now. I came over this afternoon and talked to her for a while. I told her I was looking for a room myself."

She was looking past me at the darkening water of the bay with almost the same rapt expression as years earlier when she'd proposed champagne in the East River. "I knew you'd do something like that," I said.

We walked slowly up and down the *malecón* while she told me the story of how Connie had lost a diver in the Blue Hole, a huge, virtually bottomless cavern in the shallows of Lighthouse Reef, fifteen miles offshore.

By the time she finished, she was in tears and my own eyes were puddling up. "Oh, it was so sad," she said. "She couldn't do anything to save him. She was supposed to be the farthest down, but he got below her while she was helping someone else. By the time she spotted him it was too late; he'd gotten too deep. So he just kept going. She could see him way down there in the darkness—his light, his bubbles—but couldn't do anything."

"She talked to you about all this?"

"A little. I got most of it from John."

"She could have gone down after him, but she would never have come up," I said. "It's over three hundred feet to the highest part of the bottom. She would have been narked silly with nitrogen. Even if they had made it up, they would have died of the bends."

"She watched his bubbles for half an hour," she said. "She told me that. Half an hour."

We were in front of Connie's house again. I shook my head and sat down on the seawall, facing it. "She was planning to go back to the States with him," Susan said.

"Oh, God."

"They met on the dive trip. He was a psychiatrist from Boston, just divorced."

I didn't say anything.

"This was the real thing, John said. He'd never seen her so happy."

The real thing. I cleared my throat. "How does she look?"

"She looks terrible. But she's fighting. She's surviving."

"What's she doing for money?"

Susan hesitated, then sat on the seawall beside me. I could imagine Connie inside, watching us through a louvered shutter. I tried to put my arm around Susan's shoulders, and she pulled away.

"Interesting you should ask," she said. "Don't touch me."

"I love you," I said. "Why is it interesting?"

"She wants to buy this place back and turn it into a bed-and-breakfast. She needs money to do it. Will you take your arm off me?"

I removed my arm and clasped my hands together in my lap.

"They're asking twenty thousand dollars U.S. for the house," she went on. "She figures with a twenty percent down payment she can pay off the mortgage with the profits from the bed-and-breakfast."

"What about fixing it up?"

"She's got a friend who's a contractor. He's willing to do it on spec. And she can do some of it herself."

I pulled my foot up onto the seawall, hugged my knee, rested my chin on top of it, and took a deep breath. I was beginning to feel like my friend must have felt running out of air on the Lyford Cay drop-off. "I told her I knew somebody who might front her the down payment," Susan went on. "A rich fucking American."

"A rich fucking American?" I tried to laugh. "You didn't say that."

"Oh, but I did. *Stinking* rich, I told her."

"Jesus." I wished I could see her face but her hair had fallen forward, hiding it.

Her head turned until I could see one eye. "Do you like it?"

"Do I have any choice? What are the terms?"

"To be discussed." She got up from the seawall and faced me. "I'll see you around. And by the way, I know about your little fling."

I pushed myself to my feet and reached for her hand, but she took a quick step backward and raised both of them as if to ward me off.

We stood there for a moment. It seemed like either the beginning or the end of everything—a compressed, brilliant moment one hundred feet down—except now I was out of air myself. "Susan, I can't go alone." I wasn't just talking about going into the house. "Please. Come with me."

And waited without breathing while she took three deep breaths of her own and passed me the mouthpiece.

Heroes

We made it successfully down the Mosquito Coast to Panama in June of 1990, stored the *Lord Jim* there, and flew back to upstate New York. We were aiming to reassure our families that we knew what we were doing, because we had a feeling that our life afloat was just beginning. After all, we were still together. And we were still alive—a lot more so, in fact, than if we'd stayed safely at home.

Our four daughters, their various boyfriends, and my grandson Avery (Diana was a proud mom at twenty-one) came up to the farm to welcome us back. We served wild turkey, wild goose, tofu, pasta, and *hijiki;* drank gallons of Korbel champagne; and told reassuring travel stories, featuring the Mayan ruins we'd explored, the spunky Nicaraguan kids we'd hung out with, the limpid days of cruising the barrier reef of Belize, the Rio Dulce of Guatemala, the Bay Islands of Honduras, and the lagoons of Panama.

Our daughters didn't want to hear about the bad stuff any more than we wanted to tell them. None of them appreciated hardship, though mine, I'll have to admit, didn't mind the thought of me going through some as long as I didn't bore them with the details.

"So, Mom," Page said, before dessert, "how long do you think it'll take to get the boat back to Florida from Panama?"

"Oh, just a few days. We've gotten so we can practically sail her in our sleep. Why, she can even sail herself!" She raised her champagne and smiled her best cheerleader smile. "Here's to new horizons."

Glasses clinked halfheartedly.

"The *Lord Jim* really proved herself on this trip," I said. "She's a great little boat. I think she could go anywhere in the world."

No one said a word.

"Don't give me those looks," Susan said to her daughters. "Please don't give me those looks."

The Pedro Miguel Boat Club, where we returned from upstate New York in January, is at the foot of the

Pedro Miguel locks, inland of Balboa, on the Pacific end of the Panama Canal. When the lower gate opens, the water level at the boat club rises a few inches. The *Lord Jim* would bob gently, and from the cockpit we could watch huge ships making their stately, inevitable way through, instructed by American voices over the loudspeakers. President Bush's invasion of Panama was almost a year past, and things were running smoothly again.

In the steamy evenings, tree frogs pulsed from the nearby jungle. Mercury vapor lights glowed from the locks, silent and deserted when no ship was passing through. The windows of the old clubhouse bungalow cast soft rectangular yellow light shafts through the thick air, and something (maybe Alfonso, the four-foot alligator) would splash loudly in the water across the way, where most nights we could see the club president moving past his portholes as he got ready for the night shift at some classified government decoding facility.

Many of the club members seemed to have jobs they couldn't talk about. Leary, for example, on the Westsail 32 a couple of slips down, said he was an ironworker from Boston. But how does an ironworker from Boston arrange to live on a boat in Panama? We'd seen him cleaning some kind of assault rifle in the cockpit and hadn't asked him about that either.

In February, I was summoned to New York for two weeks while Susan stayed on the boat, writing every day in the clubhouse storeroom. When I arrived back at midnight, the airport taxi turned off the main Pedro Miguel road, dropped down into the valley, and stopped under the huge rain tree that shadowed the clubhouse. The pulsing of frog calls seemed timed to my heartbeat.

I boarded the *Lord Jim* without announcing myself and clambered down into the dark salon. "Susan? Are you awake?"

Immediately a light came on in the forepeak. I could see her staring at me from the bunk; she hadn't been asleep. She was wearing one of my T-shirts instead of sleeping nude as usual. "Hi, honey," I grinned. "I'm home."

She didn't say anything.

"And I love you to pieces." Another of our favorite clichés.

"Me too. How was your trip?"

"Noisy. Why do I always get seated next to women with babies?"

"Well, come to bed. I've been working since dawn, and I feel like a wet noodle."

"I have a present for you."

"You're so sweet. Give it to me tomorrow, okay? So I can really appreciate it?"

I undressed quickly and climbed into the forepeak beside her. She was wearing shorts as well. When I moved closer to her, I felt something hard against my leg and reached down.

"Jesus. You have the fillet knife in here?"

"Sorry, yeah. It makes me feel more comfortable." She turned her back and pulled the sheet up over her shoulder. "'Night, sweetie."

I wondered about that for a while but then fell into a deep, irresistible sleep. Each of us slept well only when we were together.

I woke late, after nine, and she was already up. Through the head's porthole, I could see her standing on the next slip down talking to a woman varnishing the companionway of a beautiful old wooden sloop, a Nevins 40, I thought. I pulled on some shorts, went up into the cockpit, and waved.

She was barefoot, pushing her small feet out deliberately as she walked toward me, her long hair down now and bleached by the sun, both hands in the pockets of the khaki shorts she was wearing over a black nylon Speedo maillot I'd helped pick out in Fort Lauderdale before we left.

"Ready for breakfast?" She moved quickly past me down the companionway.

"Do you want your present first?" I went down after her and held it out, a small white box with black cursive lettering: *Cartier*.

Inside, a gold ring holding what looked like a light blue stone. "It's beautiful. What is it?" She tapped on the blue oval. "It's *plastic*."

"It's a mood ring," I announced. "Remember, from the seventies? It changes color according to your index. Blue is good, black is bad. I found it in the Village and had Cartier make the setting. So now I won't have to keep pestering you."

She worked the ring onto the ring finger of her right hand, held it up to admire, and burst into tears.

"Jesus." I put my arms around her and could feel her trembling. "It's not that nice a present. What is it? What's wrong?"

"I just missed you so much." She let her head fall against my chest. "Oh, I'm glad you're back."

I rubbed her back uneasily and whispered into her hair. After a while she let go, put on coffee, and cracked some eggs into the frying pan.

"New York has no soul," I persisted. "Unlike you." Kissing her on the sweet-smelling curve of the neck.

She reached out to flip the eggs and jostled the coffeepot, which slopped over. "I do love you, but will you sit down and get out of the way?"

I sat down behind the table and watched her mopping up the spilled coffee. With the stove on, the cabin began to seem hot and oppressive. "You're not still thinking about Belize, are you?"

"What makes you say that?"

"I don't know. Just a thought."

She took a deep breath, shoveled the eggs onto a plate, and slid it in front of me. "I've got to tell you something," she said, pouring a cup of coffee too full, then pouring half of it down the sink. Slopping sugar and milk into it, spilling it as she set it next to the eggs.

She took the galley sponge and slowly mopped the counter, back and forth, back and forth. She put the frying pan into the sink and added soap and water. "Leary and I slept together while you were away."

My two hands and the coffee mug between them now seemed enclosed in a glass box. I raised the whole thing to my mouth, took a scalding sip, and put it back down.

"There was a birthday party at the club for Benjie," she explained.

"Who's Benjie?"

"That strange little boy on the *Pandora* who's always dressing up like Batman. He's thirteen years old, if you can believe it."

"Amazing. I would have said eleven at the most."

"Or ten."

"Yeah. Maybe ten."

"But smart. What an imagination."

I just sat there.

"He's written a two-hundred-page novel." Her voice was shaking. I finally looked at her. "Anyway, they were serving Fish House Punch. Max had a recipe. He's from Philadelphia too, you know. I guess it's a Philadelphia thing."

"I never heard of it."

"Well, it's brandy, rum, and a couple of other things. It's lethal. But it doesn't make you logy. It kind of makes you higher and higher."

She'd always loved to flirt. I could imagine how she looked as clearly as if I'd been at the party myself: face flushed, eyes sparkling, hair swinging. Walking on her toes, all kinds of bon mots on the tip of her tongue.

"Somebody put on some Chuck Berry, and Leary and I started to jitterbug. He's pretty good."

I could see that, too. Leary with his long red hair, freckles, wild lopsided Peter O'Toole grin, complete with bad teeth and long-waisted, slope-shouldered Irish torso. Swinging her lightly out, pulling her back. Her eyes shining as if she were bopping with Tommy McDermott, the one Irish kid on her block in Boston, who'd taught her how to French-kiss.

The words that followed seemed unspoken, though I could see her lips move: Leary helping her back to the *Lord Jim* because by the end of the evening she was floating two feet off the ground; telling a typical Leary story in his flat, brutal South Boston accent about a childhood friend from Southie on Death Row at twenty-one for armed robbery of a Tastee Freez who requested *a b'loney sammitch and a bahttle of ahrangeade* for his last meal; then suddenly on top of her, pinning her down to the salon settee, ignoring what she said—*please, no, stop, God!*—as he very slowly, and with many false starts, pushed his way in; and at last saying something as he left that she can't remember no matter how hard she tries. . . .

"Why didn't you scream? Those people on the next boat would have heard you for sure. Or were they still at the party?"

"No, they were on their boat." She picked up the sponge again and moved it aimlessly back and forth over the counter. "I was too ashamed to scream. Can you understand that?"

"So." I didn't try to understand it, feeling the blood in my face, but seeing the coffee cup in its glass box gripped by the ivory hands of a ghost. "So. He *raped* you. Is that what you're saying?"

Her eyes were fixed on those ivory hands. Even when she whispered *yes* her eyes never moved.

"Where is he now?"

"He left a few days ago."

"His boat's still here."

"He said he was going 'downcountry' for a while. He's some kind of guerrilla."

"When's he coming back?"

"I have no idea. Not for a while." She sat down beside me, almost touching me but not quite. "I had to tell you. Do you understand?"

I shook my head. "Does anyone else know?"

She looked shocked. "Of course not!"

"Did he know I was coming back last night?"

She didn't say anything.

I could move my hands again. I covered my face with them, pressing my fingertips against my closed eyes. There were many things I didn't understand, but if Leary had been there at that moment I would have tried to kill him. I understood that better than I'd understood anything in my life.

In the late afternoon, while Susan was still working up in the storeroom, I found myself wandering over to the club president's immaculately maintained British-built teak ketch, the *Galahad*.

His bald head, dead-white face, startlingly light brown eyes (the same color as Ashley's, in fact) appeared in the companionway after I knocked on the deck. "Gordon! What a pleasant surprise. Welcome to my humble abode." And it occurred to me that all the spooks I'd met here seemed to have beautiful manners, upper-crust accents, an all-encompassing knowledge and love of yachts, and a collection of authentic native artifacts. Sure enough, below in his salon he had molas from the San Blas Islands, blowguns and poison darts from the Darien jungle, conch and triton horns, serapes from Guatemala, Miskito Indian bark tapestries from Nicaragua and Honduras.

"A cuppa?" he asked brightly, and poured from a blue-and-white Ming dynasty teapot. "And to what do I owe the pleasure of your company this afternoon?"

"Leary. In a word."

"*Mis*-ter Leary." He drummed his thin, strong fingers on the teak salon table. "A true original."

"I wondered if you knew where he is?"

The club president shrugged. "No idea. Leary goes where the wild goose goes. Why?"

"He asked me to get him something in New York. He said it was important. When do you think he'll be back?"

"As I say, no idea. What are *your* plans?"

"We might sell the boat. A lot of people do that here, don't they?"

"They do indeed. A lot of dreams die here . . . not to be melodramatic."

"Actually, what we do kind of depends on Leary. We need his help to clear something up."

He leaned back, laced his fingers behind his head, and stared at the polished brass kerosene lantern hanging from the coach roof. "I'm afraid you might be waiting a long time, then."

"You know, don't you? You know what happened."

He kept his eyes on the lantern and didn't say anything.

"Susan must have told you," I said.

He leaned forward and reached for the teapot. "I'm sorry . . . more tea?"

I shook my head.

"Did Leary ever tell you about his days in the ring? No? Ah, great days, great days. Steelworkers Hall. Real fighting, you know. Mister Leary on a good day could've spotted Clay twenty pounds and taken him in"—he snapped his fingers—"three."

"Really? We'll see how he does in court. Susan will be filing charges."

The club president sighed. "You know, when this assignment is over, I'm off to the South Seas. Seven more months, then I'm free as a bird. Do you have any idea of the legal complications here in the Canal Zone?"

"Do you have any idea how it feels to be *raped*?"

He stared at me as if I'd made a gaffe and got to his feet. "Well, it's going to take me thirty minutes to get to the office with all this traffic, so I'd best be on my way. Last year, hah—I could have made it in fifteen. That's progress for you."

The couple on the Nevins 40 invited us to dinner. Steve and Marty Sawyer; about our age, with kids in college. They were taking a year off from a contracting business in Rye, New Hampshire, to sail to the South Pacific. Steve was thin and bladelike, with steady gray gunslinger eyes. Marty was hale and hearty, loved to varnish and tell jokes: two things that would be indispensable aboard their boat. They both had salty Down East accents, sanitized versions of Leary's.

The salon of the Nevins 40 featured an inch-thick solid mahogany drop-leaf table, white painted bulkheads and cabinets with three-quarter-round mahogany trim, navy blue canvas-covered settees with white piping, and an old-style galley with a big bronze hand pump, copper sheeting, a stone sink, and a jewel-like stainless-steel gimballed Luke kerosene stove. They would never use propane, too many horror stories. Good old-fashioned kerosene is fine once you learn the system, and you can buy it anywhere in the world.

The Sawyers served tuna steaks they'd bought that day at the market in Panama City and told heroic Down East sailing stories about people like Howard Blackburn, who rowed his dory for five days in a blizzard off Newfoundland in 1883 before finally making shore, and lost all his fingers to frostbite.

"Aye, the sea makes heroes of us all," Steve said dramatically.

"But is just surviving a heroic act?" Susan asked. "Animals perform incredible acts of survival all the time. Can an animal be a hero?"

"You're right," Marty said. "A hero has got to save somebody else. Howard Blackburn's buddy froze to death, and he dumped him overboard. What's heroic about that?"

"I disagree," Steve said. "Joshua Slocum's voyage around the world was heroic. And he did it all by himself." He beat his breast gently with his two fists. "Man against the sea."

"You're all wrong," I heard myself say. "A hero is someone who stands up for what he loves and believes in, even if it means getting killed. Especially if it means getting killed." I finished my wine and poured another glass. "For example. Say Leary does me wrong. Or does Susan wrong. I fight him over it, knowing I'm going to get beaten to a pulp. But I will not quit. I keep coming back. Which is more heroic, standing up to him or beating *him* to a pulp?"

"Stand up, stand up," Steve sang. "Stand up for your rights."

"Leary would get embarrassed," Marty said. "He'd lower his mighty fists and beg you to stop coming baaack."

"And that's when I'd get him." I slammed my right fist into my left palm. "With my last ounce of reserve." Susan was sitting next to me so I couldn't see her face, but I could feel her jump.

* * *

Sleeping in clothes had become the rule for her. We'd kiss good night, she'd turn her back, and I'd put my arms around her. She was sleeping badly; I'd stay awake with her as long as I could. Now, when I heard her whisper, I wasn't sure if I was dreaming.

I whispered back. "What?"

"Please let's get out of here."

"You want to leave?"

"More than anything in the world."

I let go of her and slowly sat up in the dark. "Where would we go?"

"It doesn't matter." She turned toward me. "Let's schedule the transit tomorrow. Okay?"

"Just tell me. Did you have them send Leary away?"

"Of course I didn't. I have no control over them. I have no control over *anybody*."

"But you did tell the president?"

"He came over and talked to me the morning after the party. He said he'd seen us leaving together. He kind of knew already."

"Nobody wants any trouble," I said bitterly. "What a civilized rape."

"Are you sorry I told you?" Her voice was cold.

"Of course I'm not sorry. I just want to kill him." I felt rage pump me up to unbearable dimensions—I barely fit through the wheelhouse door on my way out on deck. From the jungle, the tree frogs sounded like escaping steam.

Then Susan was there, just behind but not touching me. "Do you realize you don't have any clothes on?"

I didn't say anything and didn't turn. I could imagine her smiling and began to feel a little ridiculous.

"I know you want to kill him, sweetie. I love you for that."

"You think he's going to kill *me*, don't you? You think I'm a buffoon."

"I hope to God nobody's going to kill anybody. That's why I want to go. It's just not worth it."

"You mean, you're not worth it?"

Still with my back to her, I could feel her turn and walk away down the deck into the wheelhouse. I could imagine her moving through the salon into the forepeak, sliding under the covers, and lying there in the dark almost under my feet with her eyes open. A light breeze ruffled the surface of the water and tingled on my bare skin.

She was in bed with the light on, reading Jean Rhys's *The Wide Sargasso Sea*. I stood awkwardly at the door, then sat down on the berth and rolled my legs in. It's hard to be dignified on a small boat.

"I'm sorry I said that. It was a terrible thing to say."

She put the book down on her belly. I could see the tracks of tears on her cheeks. "Then can we leave? Will you do it for me?"

"Susan, we can't just run. You'll regret it for the rest of your life. We both will."

"We'll both regret it more if we stay." She turned and looked at me. "We wouldn't be running away. We'd be moving forward. It all got very clear just a couple of minutes ago, after I got into bed."

"What do you mean?"

Her eyes were shining with tears and hope. "Oh, please, let's sail to Hawaii."

We'd discussed a lot of options in Panama, picking up information from other boat people, dreaming up story ideas. The least interesting seemed the milk run in the South Pacific that most people took from here: the Galápagos, the Marquesas, Tahiti . . . all the way to Australia. Also, the *Lord Jim* was a coastal cruiser, built for rough weather but not for crossing oceans. Her high wheelhouse and deep cockpit made her vulnerable, and her sail area was small. Sure, she'd crossed the Atlantic. But the Pacific was in another league, and once you were on the milk run you were virtually committed to continue.

Another option was to sail up the Pacific Coast to La Paz, in Baja California, where a friend had offered me a job running a nature expedition vessel. Another was to return to the Caribbean. The most adventurous was to sail as far as the Costa Rica–Nicaragua border and then jump off on the 5,000-mile-plus voyage to Hawaii, the longest point-to-point passage in the world.

We'd been in Panama for a month and a half since returning from upstate New York. It was now early March. By the time we started the crossing in Costa Rica it would be mid-spring, settled weather. The trades should give us all the lift we needed. Except for Clipperton Island, about a third of the way across, it was all bottomless ocean. We figured the passage would take a month.

When we got there we could reevaluate. If the boat seemed inadequate, we could sell it; the market in Honolulu was said to be strong. We could sail north to Alaska or Washington State (currents and prevailing winds virtually prohibit sailing north along the California coast). Or, if we felt good about everything and our finances continued to hold up, we could go on to Micronesia, Palau, the Philippines, Borneo, Singapore—a seldom-traveled route. Bikini atoll was on the way. The Sulu Sea. We could sail the coast of Southeast Asia, where I'd been a correspondent twenty years earlier. We could be the first American vessel to transit the Mekong to Phnom Penh since . . . whenever.

The departure of a boat is always an occasion for a club get-together, not least because getting a boat out and on its way involves moving many other boats around to make room. People pull on lines and call back and forth to each other across the canals, and the departing boat hands out cold beer.

Our boat was bow in, with two bow lines cleated onshore, two stern lines looped over pilings on each stern quarter. Susan was on the bow, ready to catch the lines when they were cast off by people onshore. I was inside the wheelhouse, at the wheel. The easiest way to cast off the stern lines was from the decks of the two boats on either side of us. The Sawyers were on one side, so they could help, but the boat on the other side was unoccupied. I was trying to maneuver the *Lord Jim* closer to that piling so I could slip off the lines myself as we went by.

I was relieved; I admit it. Scheduling the transit had taken a week, but now, on the point of our departure, there was still no sign of Leary. It was out of my hands, and as I let go of my chance to stand up to him I had a sordid little epiphany. Me getting beaten to a pulp might have been hardest on Susan. She'd invested so much in her own fantasy: me as unconquerable hero.

God knows I needed to be a hero as much as she needed to have one, but there were times when it all weighed on me with a scary, suffocating heaviness, times I realized that I was out of my depth and if the situation really called for heroism I might fail her.

I heard the shout from over my shoulder and turned. Leary was running down the clubhouse stairs, across the grass to the unoccupied boat, moving loosely and gracefully like a rugby back, and in fact that's all he was wearing—a pair of khaki rugby shorts.

He leapt aboard the unoccupied boat to cast off our stern line, and for the first time I noticed tattoos—a shamrock on his shoulder and a rose over his heart. There was writing, too, but I couldn't read it. His long hair flopped.

The piling to which our line was attached was too far to reach from the deck of the boat he was on, so he launched himself through the air and landed like a monkey, gripping it with his arms and legs. Another effortless movement, and he was sitting on top of it untying the line.

"Yo, Cap! It's Miller time!"

Suddenly what I had to do was clear. I went below.
I could hear Susan scream, hear her footsteps running
down the deck as I rooted in the locker under the port
settee. When I started back up to the wheelhouse she was
staring from the companionway as if I were carrying a
shotgun or a bomb, instead of a fifteen-pound one-foot-
eight-inch-high jeroboam of Moët & Chandon champagne my extravagant Cleveland aunt had sent us at the
start of the voyage.

"Think he deserves this?"

She didn't answer. I moved past her out to the cockpit and uncleated the starboard line to take the strain off it.
Leary and Steve Sawyer cast off their ends. "Keep backing
her down," I said to her.

Carrying the jeroboam by the neck but keeping it
hidden behind my body, I walked up the deck to the bow,
now about eight feet from where Leary sat on top of his
piling.

"Love from both of us!" I slung the jeroboam under-
handed as hard as I could at Leary's chest. He extended his
hands to ward it off until he saw clearly what it was, then
opened his hands to catch it as it slipped through, the fifteen pounds of weight overbalancing him even as he
grabbed its neck tightly with both hands, falling slowly and
silently with it ten feet from the top of the piling into the
black water.

I raised one hand to my forehead in mock salute and
turned to look at Susan. From behind the glass of the wheel-

house windows her expression was unreadable. I knew I should dive into the water myself and finish what I'd started, and at the same time I knew I wasn't going to.

I just stood there on the bow while the *Lord Jim* continued slowly back until she was clear. Then Susan put the drive ahead, and we moved out of the Pedro Miguel Boat Club without waving and without looking back.

Ah, The Sea!

Susan issued the ultimatum at dusk, after I'd climbed out of our little yellow inflatable onto the deck of the *Lord Jim*. I'd missed the sunset, staying deep in the forest to watch a pack of howler monkeys bellow and cavort in a great silk-cotton tree.

She stood over me ominously as I cleated the dinghy and straightened up with an overdone smile. "I wish you had come with me. Those howler monkeys—I was probably the first human being they'd seen for years. There were crocodile tracks on the beach. There's a spring with cold water just bubbling out of the ground. And the forest here is completely different from those jungles in the south. It's dry!"

Her mouth was a thin, straight line. "I had a great time too, sweltering on the boat. It's been almost a month since we left Panama, and every single day is the same. This heat makes me sick. I can't function in it. I hate it."

"Another reason you should have come ashore." With a teasing edge I couldn't control. "It's cooler in the forest." The heat didn't make me sick, it spaced me out. As we'd motored slowly north from the canal along the mountainous wind-shadowed Pacific Coast, I'd been entranced by the steamy, breathless calms in Panama's Golfo de Chiriquí and Costa Rica's Golfo Dulce, the baking endless palm-lined beaches on the Oso and Nicoya peninsulas. So I'd tried to loiter. This was a sore point.

"You are so fucking selfish." She pounded a fist on the cockpit coaming. "We've done everything you wanted ever since we left. *I don't want to go ashore.* I want to start the voyage."

"Susan." I threw up my hands. "This place is fantastic, and we'll never be here again in our lives. Besides, there's not enough wind to start yet." This was not entirely true. A fresh offshore breeze had been springing up as I'd rowed ashore early in the afternoon and was now steady at about 15 knots. I probably should have turned around and rowed back, but I'd rationalized that we needed to wait and make sure it wasn't a fluke.

"So now you've seen it." Her chin lifted. "If we're not out of here by this time tomorrow, I'm jumping ship."

We'd been anchored for the last two days in a beautiful deserted little cove just south of the border between Costa Rica and Nicaragua on the Golfo de Papagayo, waiting for one of the strong offshore winds the area is known for. We planned to catch its backside and ride it far out into the Pacific, where we could pick up the southeast trades. Otherwise we'd have to motor, and the cruising range of the *Lord Jim* under power was only 2,500 miles, little more than half the distance to Hawaii. For the first time we'd have to rely on the sails, but the *Lord Jim* was a motor sailer and they were undersized.

We'd laid in supplies for a month and a half and calculated how much of our 200 gallons of water we could afford to use each day. We had spare parts for almost everything and were practicing celestial navigation, because we knew that if we lost power our fancy SATNAV and SSB would be useless. Technologically, we'd be back in the fifteenth century.

But even allowing for the heat I'd been dawdling, dragging my feet. First it was supplies, equipment, maintenance, more than we really needed. I argued that everything had to be perfect for this trip. And now that the boat was undeniably ready, I'd found another excuse.

I was scared, to tell the truth. The longest voyage I'd ever made was our three-day 300-mile passage from the

Dry Tortugas to the Yucatán Peninsula. I lacked confidence. I lacked faith.

Faith, in the religious sense of unquestioning belief, is necessary for any long ocean passage in a small vessel, now just as much as it was in Columbus's day. I knew we weren't going to sail off the edge of the world, but there were other things that could happen—and had happened over the years to other people. Columbus, being the first, was operating in blissful ignorance, whereas we had many well-documented accounts of real disasters: boats rammed and sunk by pilot whales, enormous rogue waves, unaccounted-for groundings (possibly on nuclear submarines), freak storms, piracy, and arcane mechanical failures.

There were also, of course, many accounts of easy passages. They way outnumbered the disasters, so the odds were comfortably in our favor. But still, the variables are such that every ocean passage is unique, and there's no way to know in advance how yours will turn out. Like life itself.

So sailors are among the most superstitious folk on earth. You should never start a voyage on a Friday, even if it isn't the thirteenth; you should never write the name of the port of destination in your log before arrival; you should never step aboard a departing vessel with your left foot; you should never carry a pet aboard a departing vessel; you should never depart with unpaid bills. It's our way of giving faith a helping hand, and God knows she needs it.

Susan was a sailor herself by this time. She'd stood her watches alone, read charts, plotted courses. She'd maneuvered the vessel out of the way of a drifting shrimp boat in a 60-knot storm, just when it looked as if we'd be smashed to driftwood. She replaced a belt on the engine at night in a heavy sea when my back went out and I couldn't do it myself. She was as ready for the big one as I was.

Taking on the unknown had been no problem for either of us—more likely, an incentive. But since Panama things had changed.

"I'll never flirt with anyone ever again," she'd said, half angrily, half sadly, in Pavones, a surfing mecca in southern Costa Rica with one of the longest, fastest left breaks in the world. We'd had a drink in the ramshackle beach bar with a handsome young surfer from Ocean City, Maryland (who worked as an ambulance-chasing lawyer to finance his obsession), and he'd given her a little rush, even though she was obviously with me and at least ten years older than he was.

Normally a sparkle would have come into her eye, but this time she'd seemed cool and distant and let me do most of the talking. Back on the *Lord Jim*, I'd kissed her and we had our first shot at making love since Panama. It was a failure on both our sides. I'd lost faith in myself, as a man as well as a sailor. I felt I'd been shown up for what I really was: a Milquetoast who had chosen a gag with a champagne bottle over a doomed but heroic attempt at honorable vengeance. Afterward, in that same half-angry, half-sad tone, she'd said she hadn't been ready either. It had been too soon to try.

Now she needed to make the voyage more than I did. I felt superseded, almost superfluous. Maybe I dragged my feet a little just to annoy her. In some mysterious way she'd gained confidence while I'd lost it. I worried about her living in a dream world. That rage might have been driving her only occurred to me later. But rage wasn't really the answer either.

Anyway, she'd issued her ultimatum, so I reduced the whole thing to a challenge. "You know," I said, to one-up her. "If you want to, we could leave tonight. Why wait till tomorrow?"

"You said we were waiting to make sure about the wind."

"Well, it's been blowing since two. It's picked up, hasn't it?"

"Yeah, it's about twenty knots."

"It's not exactly a Papagayo, but maybe it's the best we can do."

"Maybe," she said.

"So. Do you want to go?"

She poured two glasses of wine and we made our toast, even though it was now almost dark. Then she cooked dinner while I took the inflatable apart, rolled it up, and lashed it to the deck.

In the velvety Central American night we weighed anchor, hoisted the mainsail, and bore away to sea. There was no moon; the stars shone dimly through the thick atmosphere. The course to Clipperton Island, 1,500 miles away, was a broad reach. The wind was about twenty knots. We unfurled the genoa jib, and after an hour or so, with the sparse lights along the invisible coast beginning to fade below the horizon, we shut down the engine.

We sat side by side in the cockpit, listening to the hiss of water past the hull, feeling the check and rush of the boat as the waves grew into real ocean swells.

"Takes you back, doesn't it?" I said. "Feels like we're leaving the Dry Tortugas again."

"No, it doesn't. It feels completely different."

A long silence. I felt thick and unperceptive, aching to understand who I was with now, whom I'd be crossing 5,000 miles of ocean with, my partner in survival. I wanted to reach out and touch her, to put my arm around her the way I had leaving the Dry Tortugas, but I couldn't. I wanted it to be the same, but I knew it wasn't. "So." I took a deep breath and cursed my banality. "How is it different?"

"Leaving the Tortugas was like a dream. You must have thought so too. Remember what you said?"

"I said maybe we're just in the same fantasy. And you said if it's mine, I have to promise no surprises. I've been thinking about that, as a matter of fact."

"You have? But there haven't been any surprises. At least not at sea. You've done wonderfully."

"Yeah. But I'm beginning to realize it might not be my fantasy."

"It's not anybody's fantasy. It's the real thing. I realize that now; that's why it's different."

"The real thing. How do you feel about that?"

"Pretty good, actually." She smiled encouragingly. "What about you?"

"Oh, not too bad."

She reached out and took my hand. "It's all right if you're scared. It might have bothered me on that first trip— I know it would have—but now I'd be bothered if you weren't."

I suddenly noticed her hand seemed cooler on mine, instead of warmer. What she was saying, I understood clearly, was that I had lost my hero status and was now just an ordinary guy.

"I know a lot more now," she said, letting go of my hand, standing up and bracing herself against the wheelhouse door, looking at me almost shyly. Then the SATNAV sounded its shrill beep, indicating a fix, and she turned and went inside to check. "We've gone twenty miles already," she called.

"How much farther?"

A short pause while she punched it in. "Four thousand four hundred and eighty."

I snapped my fingers and called back. "A mere bagatelle."

The wind blew a good 20 knots for three days (300 miles) and then died. There was no sign of the southeast trades. We dropped the sails and started motoring through the glassy phosphorescence-filled swells, through huge schools of bonito and albacore, occasional pods of dolphin. Boobies, frigate birds, tropic birds, shearwaters, and petrels

veered through the shiny sky. During the night, big oce-
anic flying fish hit the sails, fell to the deck, drummed for
a while, then lay in the scuppers until collected in the morning to be pan-fried for breakfast. Trolling a feather, we
caught at least one bonito or albacore per day for sashimi.
It was an ocean of plenty. The blue water glowed.

Hundreds of miles from land, it didn't take long for
the cozy reassuring routines of passage-making to narrow
the complicated, dangerous world down to a 36-by-11-foot
space that contained all our means of survival. Life became
microcosmic. We were each with the person we loved, and
sex wasn't something we missed so much as something we
didn't have time for. It was one of those rare times when
we both felt we had everything we needed.

Our main source of static was the safety harness, a
nylon web contraption like babies wear that attaches you
to the boat when working on the foredeck. I wore it only
at night and during rough conditions. She wanted me to
wear it whenever I left the cockpit, even on calm, sunny
days.

She'd never been so insistent about it before, but then
we'd never been in the middle of an ocean before either.
Still, it shocked me that underneath her newfound confidence she had such doubts about her ability to turn the boat
around in fair weather and pick me up.

In Susan's nightmares I always died and left her. A few
years before we started the voyage she'd written me one
of those letters she resorted to when she had something
important to say:

If something happens to you, does Charlie
Grimes know what to do? Because I don't. Where
do you want to be buried, what happens with your
papers, what you've written? What happens to your
things? Does Avery get the Holland & Holland? This
is not to insinuate that I have any claim on the above,
I just want to know the process, and I think that's fair
to ask.

I know this is morbid, but hell, you've been in
six airplanes in the past two weeks, often there is a
gun or chain saw in your hands, you're going to be
scuba diving, you like to take risks.

And if you think my asking to know all this is
morbid, you should be aware of my recent nightmare. Talk about sitting bolt upright in bed. The
phone call (from Bill Wood, in his vague voice). The
funeral. (In the same church as your mother's. I'm in
the third row, not family. Your family, including
Holly, is in the first row.) Fade to: for sale sign at the
farm. Me watching as the house is emptied, not only
of your stuff but mine too. Loaded into a van. Driven
away. I'm passive and voiceless in the dream.

One calm sunny day I forestalled yet another harness argument by suddenly throwing overboard one of
the buoyant white cockpit cushions. We watched it recede astern and become a white postage stamp on a vast
blue envelope.

"That's me," I said. "Now what do you do?"

We were running with the genoa poled out to starboard and the mainsail out to port before a gentle 5-knot breeze, the engine doing most of the work. Quickly and instinctively, she cut the power and started pulling in the roller-furling line to the jib while slacking the sheet. She needed all her strength, but gradually it came in until the sheet, with the whisker pole attached, was snug against the furled sail. Then she adjusted the autopilot so the boat was headed into the wind and trimmed the mainsail flat.

She looked back for the white postage stamp, but it was gone, hidden in the waves. "Oh, no," she breathed. When she turned to me for help, I felt both better and worse.

"You should have thrown the dan buoy," I said, with that teasing edge I knew she hated. "The first thing."

"*Fuck you.*"

"Can't. I'm gone."

She slapped me in the face as hard as she could, and the world disappeared for an instant, then reassembled itself from a new perspective. I said I was sorry, and I was telling the truth.

"You should be." She stared sadly at the blue, cushionless ocean. Then: "Oh! All we have to do is reverse the course! Two sixty minus one eighty . . . eighty, right?" Without waiting for my answer, she disconnected the autopilot, swung the boat to the prescribed course, and in fifteen minutes or so we were alongside the cushion. I snagged it with the boat hook. "Safe and sound."

It had been easy. She ran her hand over the dripping cushion and smiled halfheartedly. "Well, I guess if you were the kind of man who wears a safety harness all the time, I wouldn't be with you now."

I was reading *Moby-Dick* again. That evening, after dinner, I read her the chapter where Pip, the little cabin boy, panics and jumps out of a whaleboat during the chase and is picked up six hours later, totally insane. "Just don't leave me out there too long." I grinned at her.

"It wouldn't matter," she shot back. "You're already insane."

"Yeah, maybe I am," I said, still grinning. "I'm crazy about you."

She laughed and blushed like she usually did. Then her smile faded. "It would be a lonely way to die, wouldn't it? But then, what isn't?"

The next afternoon, another calm sunny one, after we'd caught up on our sleep, done all our chores, and were lounging around the cockpit like two cats, she shyly said she'd like a back rub. It was her way of saying "Let's make love." But more than that, for her a good long back rub was an essential piece of foreplay. I guessed it was a kind of fetish for developing a good fantasy, but of course she never would have admitted that.

On our way down to the forepeak, she picked out a bottle of massage oil from the medicine cabinet in the head, special stuff the Sawyers had given us to get us through what they realized was going to be a bad time. They said it was made by Hungarian gypsies and could only be bought under the counter. But until now it had sat neglected.

I opened the big hatch over the double berth that we rarely used at sea because the forepeak was the jounciest place in the boat and too wide to brace yourself. Above us, the orange-and-white- striped nylon drifter on one side and the white genoa on the other strained against a deepening blue sky. The hull gurgled and hissed in the long, easy ocean swells. Its regular movement was so much a part of our lives we barely noticed it.

Susan took off her clothes and lay face down on our cream-and-black-striped sheets. Still in my shorts, I knelt above her and squeezed a thin, clear, snaky line of pungent massage oil down and across her back and thighs. She sighed and turned her head to rest her cheek on her crossed arms. Her hair was still up, but I unpinned it, spread it on the pillow, and started. It had been so long that her body felt like a stranger's.

I fanned the embers of this fantasy until they glowed red and finally burst into flame. It was consumingly perverse and exciting—two strangers alone on a tiny boat in the middle of the Pacific. Every pore, every curve was new and different, full of unknown possibilities, and when she finally sighed, turned over, and stretched her arms toward me, I closed my eyes and concentrated on the taste and feel of a stranger's mouth and lips. I was sure she was imagining the same thing and almost asked her about it when we opened our eyes again to stare at each other. Almost, but not quite.

* * *

The farther we got from San Francisco, where the High Seas Radio station is, the harder it was to keep the schedule of family phone calls that Susan had taped to the wheelhouse bulkhead above the little Kenwood ham transceiver that we used to connect with the ATT marine radiotelephone network. She'd mailed the rotation schedule (one call every five days) out to our four daughters and her mother, along with a letter:

> We will monitor the High Seas traffic list channel daily. Call us *only* in emergency. 1800 SEACALL is the #. Tell them to put the *Lord Jim* WUR5404 on the traffic list. Estimate where we are approximately. We know *only* bad news comes to us if we are paged. If you have any news other than emergency, call the designated person for the day and tell him or her. We are thrilled to get gossip. But also remember it's $14.93 for the first minute and $4.98 from then on.

Only a few of the multitude of High Seas channels could be programmed into the ham radio's memory, and the antenna had to be retuned manually with each change, an operation that required the hands of a safecracker. If the call went through easily, and the voice of one of our daughters or her mother came lovingly and clearly through the ether, everything was roses. But increasingly it took hours of tuning for a viable frequency, waiting for a break in the traffic, only to lose out to someone with a more powerful setup (frequently a cruise ship with a long line of callers). The scheduled family member would be expecting the call, so we had to get through even if it took all day and there was only a machine to take the message.

Susan was in charge of communications, so usually she made the call, cursing, pounding the table, and hissing ironic commentary on the cozy, domestic conversations we could overhear. "Look," I told her once, when she'd been trying unsuccessfully for four hours to reach Page. "It's just not going to go through today. You tried your best, now there's nothing more you can do. They'll understand."

I never said it again. "*Yours* would understand," she answered, and her eyes were the color of Boston Harbor in February.

After the phone calls, her most important routine was the daily photograph. It was to be taken exactly at sunset, before or sometimes during the toast. Subject and photographer alternated. The subject picked the pose and the location and held up numbered cards, showing how many days of passage-making had passed.

Here too, sometimes I'd get impatient and she'd get irritated. Her fantasy included showing the photos later to exactly those same people she'd been struggling so hard to stay in touch with. The admiring looks she could imagine so clearly on their faces would finally vindicate what we were doing. They would be part of her triumph.

I realized this when I witnessed the performance back in upstate New York. The photo sequence worked brilliantly and showed me something else I'd felt but never put into words: time passes more quickly at sea than in any other environment, and the changes it made in us were there in our faces, our bodies, the boat, the ocean, for everyone to see.

Every afternoon before the sunset routine we monitored the High Seas Radio traffic list. In the second week of the voyage, more than five hundred miles from land, I got word that I was to call my stepmother, who was wintering with my father on the west coast of Florida.

My father was eighty-five, and had not been in good shape for some years. He'd had a series of heart irregularities, a pacemaker had been installed, and now he was doing little more than sitting around staring at the walls. He was almost stone deaf, in spite of two Ronald Reagan hearing aids. He'd wanted to get a little speedboat, and I'd hoped it would put a glint back into his eye, but his new wife wouldn't hear of it.

I got the call through just after dark. My father had suffered a ruptured aneurysm and was not expected to live. In the daily photograph I was seated before the radio, back to the camera, face shadowed, in three-quarters profile, tendoned hand gripping the mike. Susan had tried to hand me the numerals and, when I'd waved them away, had propped them on the chart table nearby. She wasn't going to miss this shot under any circumstances.

Whatever his shortcomings as a father, as a ladies' man he was without peer. Susan had always loved his courtly mischievous twinkle, his perfect eye for *objets,* his appetite for a savory story, his Dorian Gray handsomeness even in his eighties. In my uncharitable moments, I saw him as a kept man who'd led a purposely circumscribed life. Susan saw him as a tragic figure, an artist and adventurer manqué.

My stepmother announced that they'd had to cut off my father's right leg above the knee to keep his blood circulation up. She was crying. "I couldn't reach either you or your sister so I had to go ahead and give them permission myself. He would have died without it, but it was the hardest thing I ever did."

"I understand, Agnes," I said. "You had to do it. Don't worry about it." But the vision of my father mutilated, his body no longer perfect, was worse than imagining him dead. He himself would rather be dead than disfigured. I knew that, and Agnes did too. She'd done the wrong thing. My sister never forgave her, and she probably never forgave herself.

I suddenly knew he was gone. The amputated leg confirmed it. He wouldn't want to live. And why, I thought angrily, listening to my stepmother's voice crackle over thousands of miles of ether, hadn't she let him at least die whole?

Still, I told her we'd heave to for the night and call again in the morning. If it seemed he might survive for a while, we could be in Cabo San Lucas in a week and fly to Florida. If it was hopeless, or if he went during the night, we'd continue as planned.

One thought kept pushing its way into my mind as I sat there at the radio, bracing myself against the movement of the boat and every once in a while looking up to see Susan's tears. *Now he'll never be able to read my book. Fever Coast Log* wasn't due out till the next year, and I hadn't given him the manuscript. Some trepidation, some feeling that I wanted to present him with the finished product, a fait accompli. I'd dedicated the work to him and much of it was about him; it was my tribute to what he'd taught me, as well as a full accounting of what I felt had been his shortcomings. It was one side of a dialogue we'd never had. But really the only thing I needed to hear on his side were the British words "Well done." Finally.

The night was calm. I spent my first watch staring at the stars until just before midnight, when Susan came up to take over.

"Okay?"

"Yeah."

"Do you want anything?"

"No, thanks. Why don't you get some sleep? I'll take the rest of the watch."

She stayed up anyway, but when it came time for her second watch I didn't wake her. There was a photograph of my father I kept seeing. Wearing a pair of blue nylon trunks, he was braced in the stern of a speedboat, with the white wake flaring out behind him into the aquamarine water of the Bahamas. He was probably in his mid-forties, but his body was as fit and trim as a twenty-five-year-old tennis champion's. His usually well-groomed hair was all over the place, but what struck me most was the change in his usually reserved expression: a wild, toothy grin like Toad's in his first car ride in my father's favorite book, *The Wind in the Willows*. "Faster. *Faster.*" It was the expression of a man I would have loved to have known.

Susan took the dawn watch, as usual, while I lay in the pilot berth staring at the lightening portholes. When the first ray of sunlight refracted through the glass, I heard her scream and roared on deck, sure she'd fallen overboard. She just waved her arm at the horizon. As far as we could see in all directions, dolphins were jumping. The nearest were a few feet away, so close in the clear cobalt water the permanent smile was clearly visible before the muscles flexed and the dappled shape broke through the surface with a ripping noise and enough force to carry it ten feet up and twenty feet away. The farthest were gray specks, leaping, arching, falling. The ocean was white with splashes when they hit.

We'd seen many dolphins before. Usually they'd appear in small groups, play in the bow wave of the boat for a few minutes, breaking the surface enough to breathe, and then disappear again. This was something else.

I didn't feel her take my hand, but later Susan reminded me I'd told her many times that my father, who loved the ocean almost as much as a great meal and a fine home, had always said he wanted to be reincarnated as a dolphin. Whether the old blade really believed in reincarnation or just found the idea amusing—think of the story possibilities—wasn't all that important.

I could hear Susan saying something, and her voice was so urgent I shook my head and looked quickly down at her to see what was wrong.

She said it again, her face lit with purpose, as if she were telling me one of the most important things she knew. "Now you know how proud of you he was!"

My stepmother confirmed it when we got through to her a few hours later. My father was gone. And I assumed (though I didn't work out the exact timing) that he'd taken his leave just before the sun rose at our particular position on the globe.

The daily photograph that evening was out of sequence for the only time on the trip; she took it of me again. Later, when it appeared during the photo show in upstate New York, I was shocked to see a man who looked as different from the way I thought of myself as my father's photo had looked from the way I knew him. But we were about the same age in the two photos, my father and I, and we were both on the stern of boats with water in the background.

I do hope he was proud of me, even though he never said it. I never told him I loved him either.

Hawaii

From my eulogy to my father:

A few days later a large dark shadow appeared in our wake. It turned out to be a twenty-foot bull pilot whale . . . we could see his cows and calves rolling in the waves astern of us. And we were a little apprehensive because one of the books my father had loved was about a family's heroic survival for months in a dinghy after their sailboat had been sunk by pilot whales.

The whales had butted huge holes in the hull and the boat had gone down in minutes. We thought it was wonderful and miraculous to have my father with us, if this in fact were he, but we were a thousand miles from land, and we hoped he didn't have in mind another of his beloved survival tales, to be written by me.

The whale followed about twenty feet behind us for half an hour and then gracefully raised his flukes and disappeared. Of course we were sorry to see him go, but at the same time, I have to admit, we were quite relieved. We went below for lunch and then suddenly the boat shook as if it had run aground on a soft but muscular reef.

The whale was now about three feet from the end of our rudder. As we watched, he closed the distance and we felt the boat tremble again. The water was clear enough easily to see the dolphin-like upward curve at the corner of his mouth before he disappeared for good. But we never learned whether this last light nudge (as it must have felt to the whale) was playful mischief or just a gentle send-off and goodbye.

Not long after this, with about two-thirds of the passage left to go, we finally picked up the trades. Susan said it proved the whale's nudge was a send-off (not so gentle).

Gradually, over the next few days, the winds increased to between 25 and 35 knots, freshening just before sundown. Each time we worried whether they would grow to gale force, and, if they did, what were we going to do about it in the middle of the night, with the seas running larger than we'd ever seen them in our lives.

In the Gulf Stream, where all our blue-water experience had been, seas this large (15 to 20 feet on the face) would have been dangerously steep and probably breaking. But here in the open Pacific they were high and long and stately, their heads in the clouds, their spume-streaked faces dark with rushing cat's-paws of wind, crests feathering, curling, sometimes frothing down the faces a way before the moving energy of the wave reabsorbed them.

The boobies, tropic birds, bonito, albacore, and dolphin we'd seen in calmer waters had disappeared. The only living things out here besides us were shearwaters, cutting back and forth through the troughs and over the crests on stiff braced wings like flying knives. The deep blue sky was dotted with small low clouds like cotton swabs, sweeping across the circle of horizon that surrounded us. Puffy tradewind clouds, our sailing authorities called them.

The first few days of wind we sailed wing and wing straight before it with the drifter and the genoa out on poles, the mainsail down, and the mizzen trimmed flat to steady us, surfing down the long waves at the unbelievable speed of 9 knots, which in the *Lord Jim* was equivalent to well over 100 miles an hour in a Jeep. But the boat's motion was never awkward or uncertain—she felt as if she was doing what she was made to do—and her seaworthiness gradually made us gleeful and optimistic. We realized that in twenty years of sailing, we'd never really sailed before.

In our optimism we were reluctant to shorten sail, and at 2 A.M. one night the light nylon drifter blew out with a bang like a cannon, then a roaring flogging of tattered strips. It was my watch. I yelled for Susan. There was nothing for her to do, since we were on autopilot, unless I fell overboard from the bouncing foredeck. Then she'd have to bring the boat broadside to the wind so that the genoa on its pole would be to leeward, lower the spinnaker halyard so I could clip it to my harness—which would already be clipped to the lifeline attaching me to the boat—and haul me back on board with one of the cockpit winches, a maneuver we'd discussed and prepared for but never practiced. The 20-foot seas would have made it tricky. Still, as the boat rolled in the waves, there would be a pretty good chance I could haul myself back on board.

When Susan was ready, I turned on the feeble spreader light, clipped my harness to the thick nylon safety line running from the cockpit to the bow, and worked my way forward to the mast, where I uncleated the staysail halyard to drop the ruined sail.

Holding the halyard in one hand and the handrails on the cabin trunk in the other, I made my way to the bow. I sat down and braced myself between the windlass and the cabin trunk and waited for the flogging sheet, still attached to the clew of the ragged sail, to come within reach. The plan then was to haul the sail on board with the sheet while slowly letting it down with the halyard. Outside the cone of light from the spreaders I could see nothing. I felt like Alexei Leonov, the first man to leave the capsule and drift alone in space. I was weightless half the time as the bow fell, the other half under heavy Gs as it rose.

After that, we ran wing and wing only during the day (now with a smaller staysail on the other pole), still at incredibly high speeds, still feeling the wildness transmitted to us from the *Lord Jim*, dreaming of flying on the off watch in the pilot berth, which supported the sleeper securely on all sides like a cocoon. During the nights we doused the staysail (if the wind was average) or the genoa (if the wind was strong), took the remaining headsail off its pole, hoisted a reefed main, and headed up a few points to take the wind on the starboard quarter in a more conservative broad reach. Even so, we were making more than 150 miles a day, almost twice our average in the doldrums before Clipperton Island. Really humming along, as the old blade would say. We ran the engine only a couple of hours a day to keep the batteries up and the refrigerator cold. I was on cloud nine.

Susan has two modes of being happy. With her daughters and family she gives festive dinners and surprise presents, plays parlor games like charades and Pictionary, and sings old-time three-part-harmony pieces complete with extravagant choreography:

> By the sea, by the sea,
> By the beautiful sea.
> You and me, you and me,
> Oh, how happy we'll be.
> When each wave comes a r-o-o-o-lling by,

We will duck or swim
And we'll float and fool around the water.
Over and under and then up for air,
Pa is rich, Ma is rich,
So now what do we care!
I love to be beside your side
Beside the sea, beside the seaside,
By the beautiful sea.
By the sea!

Her eyes disappear in laugh lines, the corners of her mouth curl to inconceivable degrees, and a lock of blond hair falls across her face as she shakes her head at something Page or Ashley tells her. She jiggles and glows. She's the life of the party.

I like to think that I, alone, showed her the other mode of happiness, even though I know now she did it on her own. Her mouth opens in awe, her eyes become all dark pupil. If she talks, it's in a reverent whisper as if she were in church. This is the way she looked when we finally made it to Hawaii after thirty-five days at sea.

Starting around midnight, we'd been seeing the huge revolving light on the coast of the Big Island near Hilo sweeping across the sky. An AM country music station broadcasting out of Hilo (audible off and on for the last couple of days) sounded like it was right next door. And as the darkness finally lightened into dawn, the first things to catch the sun were the cloud-shrouded peaks of Mauna Loa and Mauna Kea.

It was my watch. I called to her down the companionway, and in a few minutes she stumbled into the wheelhouse, wiping the sleep from her eyes. I pointed at the peach-colored peaks riding above the clouds as if I were showing her the dawn of creation.

We motored in behind the Hilo Harbor breakwater and dropped anchor in calm, transparent water about ten feet deep, a few hundred yards from a pleasant cluster of white bungalows set under shady trees and green lawns. We could see tiny jewel-like fish and little crabs making their way through the eelgrass on the bottom. Cane and pineapple fields, forests, cattle pastures on the side of the mountain across the bay were slowly emerging from undifferentiated gray. We were flying our yellow quarantine flag; our plan was to get some sleep before we tied up in the inner harbor to clear customs.

I shut down the engine, and the phrase "deafening silence" began to repeat itself inside my head. Only deafness could make for silence like that—no wind trill in the rigging, no plash and gurgle of waves against the hull, no creaking of lines and parts, no engine throb, just velvety-smooth, slightly scary silence. There wasn't even any sound from shore, which was strange because we could see a few early-morning cars making their way along the causeway.

Neither of us said anything. Finally Susan sat down at the chart table, took out a blank three-by-five file card similar to the numbered ones we'd been holding up in the daily photograph for the last thirty-five days, and inked in the words WE MADE IT.

For once I didn't complain. I took the camera from the camera bag, we stepped out into the cockpit, and I propped the camera on the port thwart, facing aft. The formerly peach-colored dome of Mauna Kea, now various shades of violet and magenta, was in the background. Susan, wearing her turquoise Patagonia shirt, sat facing the camera, proudly holding the card. She hadn't offered it to me, and I hadn't asked for it. We'd both made it to the same place, but her voyage had been different from mine.

I, thirty-five-day beard, wire-rimmed dark lenses, tattered but clean gray T-shirt (she'd made me change it), leaned in from the side. Our heads touched. The automatic timer on the camera buzzed loudly in the silence, and then there was a click.

Much later, I find myself looking at the slide with a little hand-held slide viewer. My hand is shaky. My voyage *had* been different from hers, and in the future it was going to be very, very different. But what it looked like at that moment, I see now, is that we have finally gotten married. It's a wedding photo.

ROWING
IN EDEN

,,,

Outfitting

For the first time since we left Florida, there was no discussion about what to do next. Discussion implies options to consider, conflicts to resolve. There were none. We knew we would sail on to Singapore. Maybe the thing was as simple as this: we'd gotten a taste of blue water and we had to sail on. What we needed, how to pay for it, how we'd square it with our families were the only issues left.

Keehi Marine, in a blazing-hot, smoky, dusty industrial area across a shallow lagoon from Honolulu airport, was the first step. If we were going to go on to Singapore, there was serious outfitting to be done. Yard work, from the most pedestrian jobs like scraping and sanding to the most delicate and skilled, like spray painting, carpentry, mechanical installation, and repair, costs as much as a cut-rate psychiatrist, so we would do everything possible ourselves. Keehi permitted this, unlike fancier yards, and it was a gathering place for world cruisers operating on a shoestring.

We left the boat there and went back to the mainland for a couple of months to see our daughters and to talk to editors, an accountant or two, and a stockbroker. The name of our particular shoestring was DSC, an over-the-counter technology stock I'd bought years earlier. It had been a dog—I was on the verge of selling it many times—but suddenly it had doubled and was still climbing. We took out a margin loan to cover our outfitting costs because the broker said the run wasn't over. It seemed a good omen.

We both drew up lists of things we couldn't live without.

Mine:

1. Replace nonskid on decks.
2. Repair sails and hanks.
3. Replace downwind poles with socket variety, add track on mast for them with separate cars.
4. Repaint bottom, check all through-hull fittings.
5. Replace batteries with Surrette Type Ds; repair voltage regulators (one had allowed overcharging to the point of cooking).

6. Construct boom cradle for mizzen, also for use as awning support and safety.
7. Add teak cap rails.
8. Repaint deck and cabin trunk.

Susan's:

1. Fit new royal-blue canvas covers for salon settees.
2. Install Furuno GPS (Global Positioning System).
3. Install Furuno weatherfax.
4. Install Class 1 EPIRB (Emergency Position Indicating Radio Beacon).
5. Repaint head.

She gave me a hard time with the teak cap rails and repainting the cabin trunk. I gave it back to her with the new canvas settee covers and repainting the head. All this was cosmetic stuff, except mine would cost more. Still, neither of us wanted to sail 6,000 miles to Singapore in a boat that looked less than her best, inside and out. We both had a strong feeling that looks had a lot to do with stance.

The new electronics Susan insisted on came as a surprise. I hadn't been paying much attention to the latest advances. After all, they hadn't been available to the greatest voyagers of all time—Columbus, Cook, Drake, Magellan, Slocum, Robinson, and the others—and they had done just fine. Also, the authorities I most respected on modern bluewater sailing regarded modern electronics as just another thing to go on the blink when most needed. Keep it as simple as possible, they all advised. Keep it to stuff you can fix yourself unless you plan never to be far from a fancy boatyard.

Granted, we hadn't yet perfected our celestial navigation, but we were working on it; after another twenty days at sea (passage time to the Marshall Islands), it would no doubt be up to speed. Our Magnavox satnav had failed us only once so far, off the coast of eastern Honduras, and we had found the tiny island we were looking for without it. We'd become reasonably expert at weather forecasting —thanks to Watts's classic *Weather Handbook*—and planned to acquire all the printed matter available: charts, pilot charts, the NOAA data center's Mariners Weather Log, U.S. and British Sailing Directions, ocean-passage volumes, and cruising guides. And it was always inspiring to consider how this literature was a compendium of every significant voyage taken by English-speaking sailors since the beginning of the printed word.

Our radio work also was proficient enough now to quickly tune in weather information from Coast Guard stations, High Seas Radio, and the local sideband channels, decipher it, estimate its currency and applicability, and even check it out on the local ham net, if there was one. We'd informally been issued a Nicaraguan call sign when we were there, and nobody ever questioned it, though hams are notorious sticklers for protocol.

So I thought we were in good shape. But after we returned to Keehi, Susan began grilling other boat people for the latest electronic gossip. In no time at all our salon was full of magazines touting miraculous instruments that seemed to reduce everything to a matter of pushing the right button.

She explained to me how the new Global Positioning System rigs that were just becoming available operate from a finely woven network of satellites formerly reserved for the military, instead of the much coarser private network used by the SATNAV system. While the SATNAV sometimes went for hours without being able to obtain a fix from the few satellites available, the GPS has continous position information obtained from many. This information is so detailed and precise that the boat's speed over the bottom can be read off as a function of tiny changes in latitude and longitude, and its position at any given time can be determined within a hundred yards or less. Hooking this flood of data to programmed way points, an internal computer can calculate rhumb line course, great circle courses, drift or deviation from these courses, distance traveled, distance remaining.

"But how reliable are they?" I asked huffily. I was thinking that with one of these things a child could handle the navigation.

"Very reliable. Everybody at Pedro Miguel was planning to get one, if they didn't have one already. And if it breaks down we still have the SATNAV."

"How much does one cost?"

"Fifteen hundred bucks." She snapped her fingers. "But we're talking about our lives."

"If our lives ever depend on a goddamn piece of electronics, we'll be in sad shape." I was grinning and shaking my head and trying to avoid her eyes. At least some of my confidence was back.

Actually, the GPS sounded pretty good and so did the weatherfax, a near-magical device that automatically locks on to special radio signals from assorted weather stations and prints them out on paper as weather maps: isobars of varying barometric pressure showing fronts, storms, typhoons, high-pressure centers, and other salient features superimposed on a large-scale map of the forecast area—in our case, the southern part of the North Pacific. What the hell, I thought. We need all the help we can get. We just have to remember to keep everything in perspective and assume it's going to break down sooner or later. Then, if it doesn't, we'll have a pleasant surprise.

The Class I EPIRB Susan wanted was something else again. Costing as much as the weatherfax and the GPS, it sends out two kinds of signals, the first short-range on the distress frequencies, so rescue craft in the vicinity can home in on it, the second long-range to a satellite that relays the signal, along with the boat's special identification code, to the nearest U.S. Coast Guard station.

A bulky three-foot-tall six-inch-diameter orange cylinder, the EPIRB is supposed to be mounted for easy access to grab as the boat goes down. I didn't like the look of it. In my mind it seemed to be a Jonah, a bad-luck talisman, a kind of invitation for the boat to sink so it could be used.

The EPIRB debate prompted Susan's second ultimatum. We'd been back at Keehi for a little more than a week. With the prevailing wind, we were in the flight path for Honolulu airport. Conversation was punctuated every fifteen minutes or so by the earsplitting screech of modern technology, and our decks were greasy with waste jet fuel.

We'd exchanged lists a few days before, politely listening to each other's pros, rationally listing our cons, arriving at adult consentual agreement in every case but one.

During lunch in the salon after a morning's reconnoitering in electronics stores, I pointed out yet again that we already had an EPIRB—a Class 2 that emitted the short-range signals that rescue craft could home in on. What good would it be to alert the nearest U.S. Coast Guard station via satellite if the nearest station was thousands of miles away?

"You heard the salesman," Susan said. "Even if we're out of their area they can contact local rescue people."

"We can contact them ourselves. We have a radio."

"They can contact passing ships."

"So can we, a lot better than they can if they're calling from the other side of the ocean."

"We might not have time to contact anybody. Boats can go down in minutes; you know that. The EPIRB will be with us in the life raft."

We hadn't had an argument like this since I threw the cushion overboard. Unfortunately, there wasn't a similar way of resolving it.

"Susan," I said. "You know what the bottom line is, don't you?"

"Yes. Do you?"

"*The boat is not going to go down.*"

"Wrong. The bottom line is, *I'm not going on the boat without that* EPIRB."

Her mouth was thin and straight, as it had been when she'd threatened to jump ship in Costa Rica. I almost pointed out that back then my own caution had infuriated her. But I stopped, not completely understanding why.

My father's memorial service and Ashley's twenty-fifth birthday had been the two main events of our interlude back home before the outfitting. Susan's insightful, inventive gifts were always breathtaking, but for Ashley's party she topped even herself. Six months beforehand, she began soliciting written memories of her older daughter from everyone who'd ever known her. She'd put them together in a scrapbook—forty or fifty poems, essays, jingles, epigraphs, and drawings—and presented it at the birthday dinner.

I remember mostly the moment they looked at each other when Ashley realized what was inside, so touching and genuine it made me wince. I felt excluded, as from happy families glimpsed when I was growing up. Just a flash. Compared to it, though, my father's memorial service two weeks before had seemed like theater, with all of us just learning our roles.

Ashley took the scrapbook over to the couch, sat down, and began to read out loud. She laughed and cried at most of the entries (even mine), while Susan watched with such happiness I was afraid she'd catch fire and disappear from the room in a cloud of fragrant pink smoke.

Maybe it was that flash I'd had from outside the circle of happy families, embedded in some cranny of my mind, that made me close my mouth, swallow my pride, soft-pedal my superstitions, and march back to the electronics store that afternoon to plonk down $1,500 for the obnoxious orange cylinder. Maybe I realized on some level that she wasn't insisting on it for herself, or for me, but for her children. In the end, though, the choice was pretty easy. I'd rather have both Susan and the EPIRB on board than neither of them.

When we weren't working on the boat, we interviewed experts on the southwestern North Pacific, where we planned to go—the Marshall Islands, the Caroline Islands, Palau, the southern Philippines, and Borneo—en route to Singapore.

Jack Randall, a friend of my father's, was a scientist with the Bishop Museum in Honolulu who had studied and collected fishes in the area for years. He was a legend in the tiny world of ichthyology—author of many monographs and books, veteran of countless expeditions to remote parts of the world, an obsessive researcher who would brave any danger to collect a rare specimen.

My father, in his gentlemanly way, had been a part of this world. Working with a young scientist named Jim Böhlke, he'd spent fifteen years collecting and studying fishes of the Bahamas; they co-authored *Fishes of the Bahamas,* which is still the definitive text, as well as pioneered the use of scuba gear for scientific collecting. I was to quote Randall in my dedication to the second edition of my father's book (published after his death) that the old blade had "developed from an enthusiastic amateur into a competent professional." He would have been so pleased; Randall had been one of his heroes.

At a dim sum lunch with Randall, though, I sensed a coolness toward our own comparatively frivolous expedition. He'd been to Bikar in the northern Marshalls, one of the few uninhabited atolls with a navigable pass into the lagoon, but would not confirm tales we'd heard of Maori wrasse the size of coral heads, teeming fish that were so tame they followed you in the water as you walked along the untracked beach, friendly dolphins that kept the sharks away, huge flocks of terns and frigate birds. None of it was scientifically verifiable.

If we went there, he said, we had to go before the winter trades had fully established themselves in November or after they'd stopped in June. The trades piled up water at the leeward end of the lagoon, creating an unnavigable outward current in the narrow pass.

But wouldn't this schedule cut into the typhoon season? Randall answered that the area of typhoon genesis is normally west of the Marshall chain, and from there they just continue farther west. He knocked on the wooden table and grinned—"Never been in a bad storm myself"—as if people like him had more important things to worry about.

We offered to collect particular specimens he might need, if we made it in, but he said he already had everything.

Earl Hinz, *Cruising World* magazine's contributing editor for the Pacific and author of many cruising volumes, lived aboard a trawler in the Ala Wai Boat Harbor. A shrewd, foxy-looking man in his seventies, he apologized for his stink pot but said he was getting too old for sailing.

I guessed later how his foxy look had developed. Dispensing sailing advice can be tricky; the variables are enormous. It's one thing to write a cruising guide, but quite another to personally counsel people who might show up again after a disaster and say, I did exactly what you said and look what happened. *What have you got to say for yourself?*

Hinz's *Landfalls of Paradise* puts the Marshalls well outside the area of significant typhoon occurrence—less than one every ten years—although the British Admiralty Pilot puts it at one every three. He cautioned us to check with the Coast Guard and weather experts about El Niño, the huge cyclical pool of warm water off the South American coast that had been influencing weather patterns around the world for the last couple of years. There had been typhoons in or near the Marshalls in March, October, and November of 1991, very possibly a result of the El Niño conditions that prevailed.

"Might I But Moor"

Our general plan was to sail for the Marshalls as early in the coming year as possible. We hoped to stop at Bikar, if we could get in through the pass. And we hoped to sneak into Bikini, evacuated and quarantined since the nuclear tests of the forties and fifties, dive on the wrecks for the first time, and document how the underwater environment had recovered. Or not.

We couldn't leave until the yard work was done, and as usual it was taking twice as long as it was supposed to.

Repainting was the worst. Susan and I unbolted and removed the deck fittings—stanchions, cleats, winches, ventilators. Using an electric heat blower like an oversized hair dryer, we melted and scraped off the old nonskid. By hand and with pneumatic palm sanders, we sanded down the decks, toe rails, cabin trunk, wheelhouse, and cockpit. We taped the edges with masking tape and put a skirt around the hull to protect it. Then Tino, an enormous, sullen, full-blooded Hawaiian, spray-painted the whole thing with gray primer, and we started sanding again. We put on two coats of primer this way.

Finally, the *Lord Jim* was ready for the top coat of durable, costly Awlgrip. The weather wasn't, though. There were no painting sheds at Keehi, so the work had to be done outside and the weather had to be perfect: still, warm but not hot, and dry. Most days were windy, kicking up dust and grit that would stick in the paint; or else they were rainy; or both.

We'd rented a cheap room in a nineteenth-century brick tenement with arched windows in the former red-light district of Honolulu near Chinatown, a short bus ride from Keehi. After more than a month of false alarms, we arrived at the yard to find Tino donning a spray-painting suit. "Today da *kine*." Clouds hung over the mountaintops behind the city, and a little breeze was kicking up, as usual.

"Are you sure?" I asked.

"Yah." Tino looked suspiciously happy.

"I thought Curtis was going to do the painting," Susan said. Curtis was the yard foreman, an artist with spray-paint equipment but an erratic and emotional administrator.

"Nah." Looking like a yeti in his white spray suit, Tino screwed the bowl of mixed Awlgrip onto the painting nozzle and climbed up the ladder onto the *Lord Jim*. Without looking down at us, he pulled the respirator over his face, the hood over his head. He began spraying the bow, moving the nozzle in fairly precise-looking arcs.

"There's nothing more we can do here," I said. "Maybe we should take the day off. Go somewhere and celebrate."

"Keep talking."

"We could rent a car, drive over to the North Shore, and watch the surfing. . . ."

Silence, broken by the passage of another jet close overhead.

I shrugged and grinned. "Okay. What do you want to do?"

"How about going to the Royal Hawaiian for one night?"

The rambling, pink Royal Hawaiian Hotel was all that remained of old Waikiki. My parents and I had stayed there in the fifties, when the beach was still one of the world's places of enchantment and the rooms were full of newly-weds. I'd told Susan I remembered it as Honeymoon Heaven.

The hotel had recently been bought by a Japanese group and remodeled. The breezy corridors with louvered doors and room numbers on oval brass plates were now air-conditioned. But Susan and I had a room with big

French windows giving onto the garden, and when we threw them open the room was suddenly full of a smell I remembered perfectly: tangy warm salt air mixed with frangipani. Doves cooed in the garden's big hau and banyan trees, and a graceful young couple strolled hand in hand along a path. It was late morning. We were less than an hour from downtown Honolulu and Keehi Marine.

"It's just like I remember it."

Susan looked at me carefully. "Really? How?"

Sex was still not back to normal. Maybe it never would be. There was a shadow for both of us, and we had to work through it each time.

"I don't know," I said. "I can't put my finger on it exactly."

I knew if I said the word "honeymoon" it would ruin everything. Fantasies are never to be put into words.

We stood there, looking each other over. On the ring finger of her right hand she was wearing the Cartier mood ring, for the first time since I'd given it to her in Panama. I reached for her hand and held it up; the ring was blue. "Well," I said. "Looks like you're in a good mood." Still holding her hand, I thought hard about what to say next. "Do you like it here?"

A small smile. "I do."

Without understanding exactly what I was doing, I slid the ring off and looked inside the band to see the engraved letters: *Cartier.* Then I reached for her left hand and slid it upside down onto that ring finger, so all you could see from the top was the gold band.

She held her hand up and looked at it for a while, turning it this way and that. Her face was unreadable.

"Come outside for a minute," I said, and opened the door. In the dim Aubusson-carpeted corridor I tried a kiss. Her breath was sweet.

I scooped her up and carried her across the threshold back into the room, closing the door with my foot. She was trembling.

"Are you nervous?"

"Yes. Are you?"

"Very." I put her down. "Well . . . here we are."

She walked to the bathroom door and peered inside. "Maybe we should get a bottle of champagne."

"Brilliant!" I sat on the bed and picked up the phone. There were both English and Japanese letters on it.

Our bag was on the suitcase rack. She went to it and rummaged around for a while with her back to me. Then she headed into the bathroom, looking over her shoulder and waving. "Be out in a minute!" The door closed firmly and I heard the sound of running water.

A voice in my ear was speaking Japanese but as soon as I said hello it switched to English. I ordered a bottle of Dom Perignon.

I lay back on the bed and closed my eyes, over-whelmed by the strength of the fantasy. A breeze from the garden rustled the muslin curtains. Tangy, salt-smelling flowery air surrounded me. My body felt charged and tin-gling. Perfect! We were going to have our wedding night without having to have the wedding.

Marriage had always been an issue between us, mostly unspoken. A couple of months into our affair she'd written:

What I've not told you directly (plenty of innuendo, of course) is that *at this moment,* and most of the time before, I do want you to leave Holly and come with me. Well, it's out in the open now, anyway. In my journal on *Nov. 25* I wrote (and I quote), "Here's what I'll never write Gordon. I want him forever. I want to marry him. I want to wear his fucking wedding ring." It goes on a bit, and I'll let you read it. I am very scared (and I bet you are too) having written that. I'm kind of ashamed for leaving it buried, because so much of what I write, say, do, centers around that feeling. And you might as well know it.

The letter hadn't scared me at the time; it had inflamed me. Our affair was so encapsulating that the full grinding weight of its effect on others took years to make itself felt. But it did. In the end, my divorce was just as awful as the rest, and for years my daughters were pawns in a game of "Get Gordon." Sometimes even "Get Holly." Marriage came to signify heartache and enmity, and I couldn't help blaming Susan for some of it.

Susan never mentioned marriage again, but every once in a while a friend would ask significantly, "So, when are you guys tying the knot?" And I would wonder if she'd confided in them.

A knock on the door. I opened it, and a white-uniformed waiter wheeled in a frosty silver ice bucket containing the Dom Perignon. A creamy linen napkin, matching the tablecloth, looped around its neck. I tipped him five dollars, and he bowed and left.

Water was still running in the bathroom; it seemed to have been running for hours. I went and knocked on the door. "Sweetie, the champagne's here." When she didn't answer, I slowly swung the door open.

Steam from the shower made everything loom and glow. Susan, nude and bright pink, was sitting on the closed toilet seat with her chin in her hands and her elbows braced on her thighs, staring at me, shaking her head.

"Jesus! What's the matter? What's wrong?"

"I just couldn't make it work."

"What do you mean?" I felt a stab of panic. "It was working perfectly."

"You're so sweet," she said. She'd been crying: her nose was slightly swollen and her eyes were red. It made her look wonderful.

"I'm not trying to be sweet. It was a wonderful idea."

"Oh, God, don't say that."

"Why not, for heaven's sake?"

"Because it was the stupidest idea I ever had."

"It was working for me," I said, beginning to feel stupid. "It felt right."

She got up from the toilet seat and walked toward me, glowing in the steam, the humidity making her hair curl and her puffy eyes shine. She put her damp, warm arms around my neck, pulled my head down, and kissed me.

After a time I put my mouth close to her ear and whispered, "Doesn't it feel right?"

The ice had melted in the ice bucket and the champagne was warm. We called room service and asked for a cold replacement, and they agreed without any hassle.

"So. What happened in the bathroom?" I asked, while we waited.

"Nothing in particular. I just lost it. You know?"

"Oh, come on. There must have been something. Just this once, will you tell me?"

"Well." She couldn't hold back a smile. "If you must know, I didn't have anything to wear. I didn't have a goddamn trousseau. I was thinking about wrapping myself up in one of the curtains, but that would have been pathetic."

"No, it wouldn't."

"Anyway. So then I started thinking about everything."

"And what conclusion did you reach?"

"Well, that's when I started to cry. It felt so good I just kept on and on. Until you came in."

"And ruined everything."

"And rescued me."

The same waiter, nodding politely, appeared with another ice bucket and another bottle of champagne. He replaced the warm one with the cold one, his eyes averted from

Susan in the bed and me in a towel. I tipped him ten dollars. We poured the glasses and carefully touched them together.

"What time is it, anyway?" Susan asked. I noticed she'd turned the mood ring around so that the plastic oval showed again. Clear blue. But it was still on the ring finger of her left hand.

"Let's not look," I said.

"Do you think it feels different since we got here?"

"Here to the hotel? I'd say so."

"Well, yes. But I meant, since we got to Hawaii."

"What?"

"Between us."

We lay there, sipping the champagne and inhaling the breeze. Hindsight is a terrible thing. Hell, in fact, is knowing that you should have done it differently. Instead of sidling around the point with a slightly clumsy, perhaps endearing rejoinder, what I should have said (how many times have I gone over this?) was this:

Listen. There's a church on the windward side of Maui. I saw it when I was here with my parents driving on this twisty narrow road along the cliffs. It's on a piece of flat ground that sticks out into the ocean with a few trees and old black lava walls, but mainly amazing green fields surrounded by this deep blue water breaking on black rocks. The church is quarried limestone or lava. It looks old and kind of overgrown. Maybe abandoned. Nobody's mowed the grass in a while. Anyway, the minute I saw this church I understood that it was important to me. . . . I mean, I still have this perfectly clear image of it in my mind even after thirty years. Now I think I know why.

At this point, Susan would ask why.

Because we're supposed to get married in it. I mean, if you want to.

Here maybe I get down on my knees.

Do you?

I can see her face.

Instead of flying to Maui the next morning, we took a cab to Keehi. The *Lord Jim* was sitting there gleaming in the mid-morning sun. She looked ready for anything.

When we climbed aboard to inspect the work, though, we could see that the new priceless Awlgrip was rough with pieces of dust and grit and so unevenly laid on that in many places the primer showed through.

"Oh, God," Susan said. "This is shit, isn't it?"

"Yeah. But we can still leave. It doesn't have to be perfect."

"What about the money?"

"We'll refuse to pay the full price."

"Do you really want to sail to Singapore looking like this?"

What could I say? Down below, we saw Curtis walking toward us and trying out a smile. "How's it look?"

"Come on up and see for yourself," I said.

Curtis climbed the ladder and knelt on the deck, running his hand over the paint. I showed him the spots where the primer showed through.

"We thought you were going to do it," Susan said.

"Tino wanted it so bad I let him try it."

"You let him learn on our boat?"

"Well, not exactly." Curtis was fidgeting like a school-boy.

"So what do we do now?" I said, after a little while.

"Sand it down and put on another coat," Curtis said, looking at the sky. "I'll put it on." He tried to look at us, failed, coughed. "Okay? I'll get Joe and Tino to give you a hand with the sanding."

"No you won't," Susan said. "Tino's never getting on this boat again."

"Joe and Larry, then," Curtis said, trying to give a jaunty salute as he put his foot on the first rung of the ladder to beat a retreat.

By the time the second coat was on, it was too late to leave. As we knew, the typhoon season in the western North Pacific starts in May, reaches its peak in late June through early October, and tapers off in late November, though typhoons can and have occurred at any time. If we left now, in March, we'd have only a month of clear sailing. The Caroline Islands, our destination for this leg, are on the edge of the typhoon belt.

We decided to return east to see our families, hustle writing projects (Susan was still at work on her novel of the Mosquito Coast; I had a Mexican novel in my drawer that I didn't want to give up on), and come back in the fall. The doggy technology stock DSC that would finance this, meanwhile, had tripled. And once again, we saw that as a favorable sign.

* * *

But the yard bill, when I got it from the office, left us gasping for air. By far the biggest item was the paint job. We'd been charged for both coats of Awlgrip, Tino's lousy job and Curtis's excellent one.

Tommy, the taciturn Hawaiian yard manager, listened while I went through our list of grievances, then grunted. "You finished?" That was all he said.

Susan had made friends with Lisa, a big, blowsy blonde who ran the mail room as a kind of gossip center—cum—parrot jungle. Lisa told her that the yard was in the process of being sold to a group of Japanese investors, like everything else on the island of Oahu. Susan got the name of the group's executive officer and his phone number. "I think we should talk to him," she said.

"I don't think it'll do any good," I said. "What do they care about us? They're probably going to turn the yard into a shopping mall."

"Well, I think it's worth a try. We couldn't be any worse off than we are."

I told her she was welcome to it, if she wanted to handle it herself. I had other problems. The boat was going back in the water, but the yard had notified us there were no slips available. Boat space in Honolulu was so scarce and expensive there was a flotilla of transients anchored illegally in Keehi Lagoon.

Susan called the number and was miraculously granted an appointment. While I canvassed the neighborhood for affordable dock space, she compiled from her daily diary a complete accounting of every man-hour of yard work, including those we'd put in ourselves. I went with her to the appointment, though we agreed she'd do the talking. When we came out, we had free dock space at Keehi for the next six months, and half off the yard bill. Tommy, the yard manager, was fired a few days later.

Portents

Hurricanes were in the news that year. In late August, Andrew swept through South Florida and Louisiana with winds up to 175 miles an hour, killing sixty-five people and doing twenty-five billion dollars' worth of damage. Andrew was reported to have been the most destructive storm in U.S. history.

A little more than a week later, as we watched helplessly from upstate New York, Hurricane Iniki roared in from nowhere and took dead aim on Honolulu. The rigger who had helped install our new downwind whisker poles had to talk his way past roadblocks to get down to Keehi to secure the *Lord Jim*; the entire area was being evacuated. But at the last minute, Iniki turned sharply and came ashore on the island of Kauai, 70 miles northwest. Like Andrew on the mainland, it was the worst storm ever recorded in the Hawaiian Islands.

The *Lord Jim* felt only a brisk 40-knot breeze. We took this as yet another good sign.

We returned to Keehi in early October, and Susan immediately scheduled more interviews with weather experts at Coast Guard headquarters and at NOAA's Ocean Services Department. She asked them if El Niño conditions still obtained, and what they thought about a departure for the Marshalls later in the month, putting us there in mid-November before the trades kicked up and made entrance to Bikar's lagoon impossible.

Both the Coast Guard and NOAA said that the El Niño conditions had dissipated, and both gave us a green light. We left on October 17, 1992, and as we slipped down the fall trades toward the Marshalls we could see on our new weatherfax at least one tropical storm marching across the chart ahead of us on an almost due westerly track. We congratulated ourselves at having left late enough to miss it.

Susan wrote two letters before we left. One she photocopied and sent out to all family members. I told her it encouraged even me.

Hi Everybody!

This letter could be pretty boring unless you are an electronics freak. . . .

Our EPIRB (Emergency Position Indicating Radio Beacon) is a class 1 and operates on a 406 frequency, which provides a coded signal that allows the *Lord Jim*'s registration to be identified. It has two other frequencies: 121.5 and 243 megahertz. All three are used by COSPAS/SARSAT satellite systems; 121.5 is monitored by commercial aircraft and by search-and-rescue craft. This is the *best* EPIRB (see attachment EPIRB). "Mad Dog" Blauenstein from the USCG was my adviser on this.

We just bought a Furuno GPS Navigator (Global Positioning System). A constellation of satellites placed in nearly 20,000-km-high 12-hour circular orbits provides precise, continuous, worldwide, all-weather position, plus time and speed. The GPS backup is a SATNAV (also v. accurate). If the electronics fail, we have a sextant and will navigate by the heavenly bodies.

We also bought a weatherfax (Furuno). This provides highly accurate forecasts for 48 degrees and good forecasts for 72 degrees. With the help of Lt. Josh McDowell from the elite NOAA Ocean Services Department of the Department of Commerce we have learned how to interpret surface windstream, tropical surface, and land surface analyses. (Analysis is officially abbreviated ANAL.)

We have a recently inspected Zodiac life raft and an extremely well-equipped and stocked emergency grab bag.

The *Lord Jim* is in tip-top ship shape, and so are *we*!

The other letter was to me, but it stayed in her drawer up at the farm. I didn't read it until later:

Dear Gordon,

I'm scared about the upcoming trip for the following reasons:

Weather: Seeing the hurricane in Hawaii scared me.

Dangerous situations: You without safety harness. Even though you promised when I agreed to go on the Maine trip to wear a harness when I asked you to, I do not believe you. I do not trust you.

Diving at Bikar atoll: I think it is foolhardy and the prospect terrifying. I am a complete novice and you have had the bends. You will be excited and your judgment will suffer.

The thing that scares me the most is that you will continue to choose not to listen to me when I voice my fears. You don't care if I am scared. You don't stop teasing when I beg you to stop. You ridicule and denigrate my concerns and act as if they are not real. They are very very real.

I am a fearful person. I try to overcome fears all
the time. I think I do brave things. I do brave things.
I don't want to do careless, stupid things.

When I finally read this, my first reaction was exactly the one she hated: to try to dodge, to sidestep, to
avert my eyes. To rationalize that she hadn't sent it because she realized it was bad-tempered and overstated. To
contrast its timidity with her intolerance of my own in
Costa Rica. Anything I could think of not to face those
sentences.

Listen to how contradictory she was, and how hard
to understand:

She was a great mom, but once told me that it
helped to pretend she was in a movie.

One of her favorite books was *The Story of O*.
Another was *Sue Barton, Student Nurse*.

One of her favorite games was poker. Another
was charades.

One of her favorite activities was to dance by
herself late at night. Another was to collect bones.

She was terribly afraid of cows, whales, or
anything large, no matter how harmless, but loved
being out in the middle of the ocean.

She hated speed, even the low speed of our
inflatable, but loved to go on the scariest amusement-
park rides.

She hated falling, diving, jumping, or anything that involved losing bodily contact with the ground, but loved to fly.

One of her favorite poems was Emily Dickinson's cryptic "Wild Nights." She'd written it into her journal, in a passage about a previous lover:

Wild nights! Wild nights!
Were I with thee,
Wild nights should be
Our luxury!

Futile the winds
To a heart in port—
Done with the compass,
Done with the chart.

Rowing in Eden!
Ah! the sea!
Might I but moor
Tonight in thee!

A fearful person? Our worst moment together so far had been in the air, not the sea. The second summer after I got my pilot's license we rented a Cessna 172, a heavy four-seater that handled differently from the two-seater I was used to, and flew it from our place in upstate New York to a little strip near the beach at Plum Island, Massachusetts. By the time we got there, in the late morning, a strong crosswind had kicked up off the ocean.

To land, you have to drop in close over the tops of some tall trees, which act as a windbreak so that the corrections you've been making suddenly become overcorrections. You have to get the plane straightened out and down fast, because the runway is short.

I blew off two approaches halfway through the final leg, giving the plane full power, gradually taking off the flaps, and going around again. We'd been coming in too high and fast, or too low and slow. Susan was calm, but with each go-round I worried more about how long her calmness would last.

We were too high and fast again on the third try, but I decided to go for it anyway. I pushed the nose down after we'd cleared the trees and approached the runway at something more than 70 miles an hour.

I wanted to get it down and get the brakes on, so I didn't flare as much as I should have, and the nose wheel touched first. The nose bounced back up into the air and the plane took a long hop. Instead of pulling the wheel back and stalling it out, I pushed the wheel forward to guide the plane back down to the ground. The nose wheel hit first again.

The second hop was higher and steeper. There was a third hop and then a fourth—worse every time—until I finally remembered to pull the wheel back and stall out. We hopped off the runway like a giant cricket and came to rest on the grass border.

We looked at each other. "Well," I said. "That's called porpoising."

Susan nodded matter-of-factly.

"Are you all right?"

"Yes. Are you?"

I nodded and tried to grin. It was beginning to dawn on me that our flying together was finished for good. She would never get in a plane with me again. And I would never ask her to.

Taxiing back, it became obvious that the nose wheel had blown out. We turned into an empty tie-down slot and shut down the engine. A big handsome blond guy came over after we'd climbed out and were standing a bit shakily next to the plane. He had a military stride.

"Who was flying that airplane?" he barked, looking at Susan.

"I was," I said. "It was all my fault."

He focused on me then. His eyes filled with disgust. "That was the worst landing I ever saw. A disgrace." He went about tying down the Cessna as if it were his.

"Do you have a spare tire for the front wheel?" Susan asked.

He stared at her for a long minute, and his expression changed. "Maybe. But I'm afraid this plane's not taking you anywhere until this pilot's been thoroughly checked out. If he wants to go by himself, that's his business. But he's not risking anyone else's neck at this airport."

"Well," Susan said, "we were planning to spend the night with relatives anyway. Do you think we can get all that done by tomorrow?"

How I loved her for that. Her expression never changed. I loved her calm face and her steady eyes. I loved her courage and the mystery of where it came from. But most of all, I loved her for backing me up.

It was only years later, after I read the letter hidden in her drawer and compared it to the letter she sent to her family before we sailed from Hawaii, that the cost of Susan's courage became undeniable. I could no longer overlook how hard she had to struggle to overcome her secret fears. And this was painful because of course I'd known all along that I was one of them.

Paradise

On November 9, just before sunset, we dropped anchor in the lee of one of the little islets strung like pearls along the encircling barrier reef of Wotho atoll, in the northwestern Marshalls. I could see the anchor lying on white sand 15 feet below the boat as if I were looking down through air. Terns and frigate birds were floating like fish in a golden liquid element around the palms overhanging the little beach, while surf from the open ocean where we'd been an hour earlier broke blue and white on the reef outside.

Susan shut down the engine, walked up the deck, and joined me on the bow. The boat was eerily steady and quiet. From what seemed a vast distance came the trafficky sough of the surf and the high, wild cries of the terns.

As the light deepened and the colors intensified, Susan whispered, "This is paradise. And you made it possible."

Any decent spiritual travelogue will tell you that you don't find paradise on purpose. If you're living right, it just happens. One day you look around, and you're there.

We'd made our first landfall in the Marshalls at Bikar, as planned, but the current in the narrow pass had been too strong to risk an entry. We'd heaved to for the night, waiting for slack water, and a trailing jib sheet had fouled the prop. It froze with a heart-stopping crash, yanking the shaft back several inches, loosening the stuffing box, and even bending the engine mounts.

We were taking water through the box, though the bilge pump could handle it, and after I cut the rope away (not easy in 10-foot seas) the prop was still functioning. We needed to get somewhere to make repairs, and since the current was still too strong through the Bikar pass, Wotho—about 270 miles southwest—was one of the closest along our route. From the chart and the pilot, entry looked easy enough, and there were some nice protected anchorages. In 1962, according to the pilot, the population of Wotho was 56. Our tourist guide reported that in the old days Marshallese royalty had favored it as a vacation spot.

Wotho Lagoon is a rough oval, about eight miles across at its longest point. We entered through the southern pass and anchored at the far end from Wotho Island, where the village is, because we wanted to indulge a feeling that this atoll, like Bikar, was uninhabited. The village was well out of sight. We were alone.

I hung the swimming ladder, stripped off my clothes, and dove over the side. The water was cooler than the humid air, with a silkiness I hadn't felt before anywhere. About ten feet down I opened my eyes. The evening sun made the water peach-colored, like the sky.

Still underwater, I swam to the anchor chain and hung there, holding on. I felt no need to come up, as if I were absorbing oxygen directly from the water around me like a frog can. The silk played around every part of my body.

I let go finally and rose to the surface without swimming. Susan was at the rail, smiling down at me.

"You look like a fish. In your element."

"Jump in. There's something amazing about this water."

"What about sharks? Don't they come in at sunset?"

"Do you see them eating me? This is paradise, don't forget. You live forever."

"Do you just get older and older? That sounds awful."

"Of course not. You stay any age you want."

"Okay. I'll settle for twenty-eight."

"You've got to get in the water, though. It only works if you're in the water."

Almost shyly she stepped out of her shorts. Still in her T-shirt, she reached through the wheelhouse window for a barrette. When I begged her not to pin up her hair, she put the clip back and pulled the jersey over her head. Her breasts always surprised me. They looked like Marilyn Monroe's—cheerleader, Hollywood, 1950s breasts.

It was now the 1990s, and we were both middle-aged. But boat life is better than Elizabeth Arden. Joshua Slocum was fifty-four when he finished his epic single-handed round-the-world voyage in 1898 and wrote:

> Was the crew well? Was I not? I had profited in many ways by the voyage. I had even gained flesh, and actually weighed a pound more than when I sailed from Boston. As for aging, why, the dial of my life was turned back till my friends all said, "Slocum is young again." And so I was, at least ten years younger than the day I felled the first tree for the construction of the *Spray*.

I watched Susan carefully descend the swimming ladder. From the back, she was smaller and more rounded than Marilyn Monroe. More domestic. More vulnerable. More lovable.

She put a toe in the water, sighed, and committed herself, looking at me with a little wrinkle of worry on her forehead as if even now she wasn't sure she remembered how to swim. Her long hair spread out from her shoulders. "You're right," she said breathlessly. "This water is amazing."

"It feels different, doesn't it?"

"Yeah. It feels . . . safe." She looked surprised.

I exhaled a little and pushed myself underwater with a couple of upward hand strokes. Her body glowed in the slanting light beams, her breasts high and weightless, her belly a pale moon tapering to a dark triangle and dark tanned legs, her hair floating up.

"God," I said, when I resurfaced, "you're a mermaid."

Jury-rigging the stuffing box to stop the leak turned out to be easier than we'd thought. A complete repair would mean remounting the engine, but that would have to wait. We could get by, at least until Ponape.

But once you find paradise, you don't want to leave. Who knows when or if you'll ever find it again? Under the boat, ample proof that God is an artist, were pastel reticulated brain corals, fire corals, plate corals, five-foot-wide anemones filled with giraffe-maculated brick-and-white clownfish, Kabuki-like but deadly poisonous lionfish. And farther out, nimble inquisitive gray reef sharks, wary dolphins, blundering graceful sea turtles, hundred-pound blue-green Maori wrasses, and giant tridacna clams with soft brown neon-spotted lips and intricately chambered opalescent interiors. (Like all explorers, we were prone to lists.)

Around noon on the second day, the village launch showed up with the mayor, who asked us for our clearance papers and cruising permit, which of course we didn't have. We were the first yacht here he could remember. He looked dubious when we explained that we were here for emergency repairs and showed him the jury-rigged stuffing box.

The launch took us in tow to the village, where he radioed Majuro for advice. Then, smiling beatifically, he told us we could stay as long as we liked, go anywhere, do anything. He handed Susan a cardboard box and opened the lid to reveal a giant crab. "Him good eat. Welcome to Wotho."

The crab lived on coconuts, husked with its powerful claws. It had a large soft body, almost like a hermit crab's without the shell. That evening we poached it carefully, and the meat had a tender coconut flavor. It was heavenly.

As soon as we went ashore a group of girls attached themselves to Susan. Holding her hand, they led her around to places of interest, taking down her long hair to comb or braid it, giving her coconut candy, ripe breadfruit, papayas, pandanus baskets, and coral trinkets and teaching her Marshallese words and songs in return for English ones. She learned all their names, forgot them, and had to be told again. They never got tired of her. "I can't believe how sweet they are," Susan said. "They're angels."

We decided to write a piece on Wotho but to use a different name and not reveal exactly where it was. To name it would have been almost blasphemous. Wasn't it enough for people to know a place like this was out there, and they could stumble on it by accident themselves?

I explored and catalogued the reefs, the lagoon, and the uninhabited islands while Susan learned the lore of the village. In a soft, effortless procession the days slipped by like tradewind clouds. We were sustained by what I could catch in the sea and what the villagers gave Susan: crab, clams (a smaller species, related to the tridacna, which tasted almost as fine as abalone when sautéed), conch, snapper, and more fruit. We never argued anymore; there was nothing to argue about. The issues between us resolved themselves or faded into insignificance.

Time was different here. We had a feeling it could go on forever.

WILD NIGHTS

Typhoon Gay

We were watching the sky, where the storm would come from.

In the morning, hazy cumulus clouds shot past, alternating with searing blasts of white sunlight. The air glowed with humidity, and quick, luminous terns rode the damp currents like trout. Our skins were shiny and sticky and we were always a little short of breath.

"I feel like a frog," Susan said. "I smell like a frog."

"How does a frog feel?"

"Permanently damp."

"How does one smell?"

"Aquatic. Fertile. Kind of like a pond in summer."

"We're in the same boat," I said, sniffing.

"Luckily," she said. "I better not kiss you, you might turn back into a prince."

By midafternoon the clouds had thickened and turned gray. The air currents had settled down and were moving with steady force across the surface of the lagoon. The formerly electric blue element now matched the air in color, except for small, luminous whitecaps that stood out as strongly as the terns had a few hours earlier.

The wind was pouring through the gray coconut palms of Wotho Island, making them writhe like water plants in a strong current. Kids played excitedly on the grayish-yellow beach. We saw the minister in his white long-sleeved shirt come out of his cinder-block house, look at the sky, look out across the 300 feet of clear, warm, choppy water that separated him from our vessel, and wave. That morning, after we'd gone ashore and Susan was off with her girls, he'd said she'd be welcome to spend the night in the church—along with himself, his wife, and his congregation. He knew better than to invite the captain.

I told Susan about it as we were walking down to the dinghy. "Give it some thought," I'd joked, knowing that she wouldn't. "If anything ever happened to you, I wouldn't want to be the one to have to tell Ashley and Page."

The moment didn't seem important. The storm was going to miss us, we were sure it was. And there was a lot of work to do to get the boat ready. I needed her help.

It wasn't as if we were far from land. I could row her in later, after the work had been done.

If things looked bad.

If she wanted to go.

If I thought she should go.

We were stripping the *Lord Jim* of everything that might catch the wind: sails, sheets, awnings, dock lines, fenders, the boarding ladder. We stowed everything below but the life raft and four large plastic bags of trash and garbage up on the wheelhouse roof.

The bags had been accumulating since Hawaii and some of the garbage was pretty ripe, but Susan had refused to let me bury it under the palms of the deserted island where we'd been anchored. Our first argument since coming to paradise.

The bulky brown bundles were in a different place when I came up from the cabin after stowing a load of gear—aft of the cockpit, in a little eddy of wind that curled around the wheelhouse and blew the smell back inside it. They rose high over the cockpit combing, hid the dock lines, and made it hard to get to the dinghy.

"I moved them down there so they wouldn't blow off," she said.

I opened my mouth, thought better of it, closed it—
and opened it again. "They'll blow off anyway. Look at
them."

She never turned. "Fine. If they blow off, they were
meant to blow off. At least it won't be us doing it."

I threw up my hands and thought, *She has no idea how
bad it could be.* But later, when I'd had a chance to think
about it a lot more, I realized that she might have had a
better idea than I. Worrying about the garbage was her way
to cut the storm down to size.

It was nothing short of miraculous to everyone who
knew us that we'd managed to survive so much time together alone on a small boat. We'd had our spats—that
morning, when she'd been unable to remove the mizzen,
I'd suggested that after three years of living aboard she might
have learned how. "You never showed me how," she'd
shot back. "You never show me anything because you want
to keep me helpless."

Helpless! First I'd laughed in amazement, and then I'd
apologized. Yes, she was small of stature (about five foot
four), but she'd been fired from at least one job for feminist militancy, had kicked an armed mugger out of her car,
had thrown her husband out of their house for philander-
ing, and almost jumped ship in Costa Rica. I admit I pushed
her out of a dinghy once, but that was nothing compared
to the Silent Treatment, her favorite weapon.

Sooner or later, though, we'd rediscover how much
we loved what we were doing and how much we needed

each other to make it work. Our love for each other flour-
ished on the boat as nowhere else. All the extraneous elements were gone. There was just us between the sky and
the water, and our tasks were clearly delineated: to help
each other survive and make it over a new horizon to the
next port.

The rushing grayness all around us was deepening into
dusk as I put on my mask, snorkel, and fins and jumped
overboard to check the anchors. The wind now was well
over 20 knots, but we still had a good lee from the nearby
island and the water wasn't too rough. It was as warm as
the air or warmer, comfortable and reassuring. Angelfish
and wrasses were playing near the bottom, glowing like
jewels in the dim light.

Both the 45-pound CQR plow on the three-eighths-
inch chain rode and the 40-pound Danforth on the three-
quarter-inch nylon were well buried in soft mud, a great
holding bottom. If the wind shifted, and it probably would,
the boat had room to swing 360 degrees without coming
close to coral.

The water felt so luxurious I didn't want to come out
into the wind. I floated on my back, kicking slowly, enjoying its movement past my skin. The Lord Jim lay nicely to
the two rodes, and Susan watched me from the wheelhouse.
I took a few deep breaths, jackknifed my body to raise my
feet in the air, and slid down toward the bottom 20 feet away.
I moved slowly, so the fish wouldn't be alarmed, and headed
back to the boat underwater about a foot from the bottom.

* * *

The 6 P.M. weatherfax from Honolulu came over clearly. Typhoon Gay was about 120 miles east-northeast and moving west-northwest at 7 knots. Maximum winds were 80 knots. When we tuned in WWVH, the powerful radio station in Kauai, Hawaii, that broadcasts time signals twenty-four hours a day for navigational purposes and emergency weather reports every hour at exactly forty-eight minutes after the hour, their report coincided with the weatherfax. Things looked good.

Four days earlier, when we'd first thought about leaving Wotho for Ponape, 480 miles southeast in the Carolines, an ominous low-pressure area had been hanging over the open water we had to cross. We waited another day; the low-pressure area divided like an amoeba. One of the new nuclei began to drift up to the northeast, in our general direction. Toward the end of the day it had become a tropical depression, with winds around 30 knots.

The next day it had reached the islands a few hundred miles eastward and intensified to a tropical storm, with winds up to 60 knots. We assumed it would now follow the usual storm track northwest and decided to wait until it was safely out of the area. But instead of moving out, it zigzagged north and south and continued to intensify.

When it finally resumed the storm track sometime in the middle of the night, it had become Typhoon Gay. Waiting it out still seemed best; our anchorage was protected to the north and east by the island and the curve of the reef. The track would take it more than 60 miles to the north of us. Winds at Wotho shouldn't be much stronger than the last storm's, where our two-anchor system had been more than adequate. There were no other boats around to break loose and drift into us. If we sailed south away from the storm, the winds would be less strong but we'd be in open ocean—at night.

Stripping the boat had made a big change in the way she rode. "I bet the wind's over thirty knots now, and she's perky and buoyant as can be," I said. "Just like you."

Susan was wearing a dark green tank top, over a black bra, and the pink jogging shorts she'd bought in Hawaii for our daily run in the park near Keehi Marine. Her hair was loose and windblown.

We were alone in the still-grayish darkness, although on shore we could now see the flickering kerosene lamps of the village and the single battery-powered electric light at the community center. No matter what, the night was going to be long and dark, and without her, after all those other nights we'd been through together, I would have felt only half there.

"I'm glad you're not ashore." I put my arms around her. "Really glad." Her body was warm and soft and smelled of sun and suntan lotion; her hair tickled my cheek. When I looked down at her, her eyes were closed.

"I am too," she said, a bit absently. "Listen, I really should call Ashley and Page. Page has probably been tracking this thing. She tracks all of them."

I groaned. We were out of range of High Seas Radio in San Francisco and had to place our calls now through Sydney Radio in Australia. Even in the best of weather the routine was long, complicated, excruciating. "Couldn't we call them all after the storm?" I said. "Please?"

She finally agreed. We uncorked a bottle of cold California Gewürztraminer from the refrigerator, poured ourselves glasses, looked at each other, toasted, and drank. The rising wind in the shrouds made a little trilling sound every once in a while, like a songbird, and the faint but somehow reassuring smell of the garbage curled through the cabin.

"Well," I said, "I guess tomorrow we'll know what we should have done, won't we?"

We heated up two cans of extra-hot Hormel chili while the wind rose steadily and backed into the north, so we were no longer protected by the island. By 9 P.M. the sustained force seemed to be approaching 50 knots (not that easy to judge in the dark with no anemometer) with gusts over 60—stronger than anything we'd been through before. The 9:48 weather on WWVH hadn't been updated, so we assumed there hadn't been any major changes in the storm's direction or intensity.

We called the village radio and asked them what they'd heard. They said the storm was due to pass at around midnight or a little later. We drew its projected course on our chart and figured that the wind might get a little stronger, but not much. I went up on the bow to check the anchor lines, adjust the antichafe guard on the nylon one, and let a little out so that as the boat swung farther into the north the strain on both rodes would remain the same.

As soon as I got out there, it seemed, the wind picked up. It whistled in my teeth and blew a tune through my nose. Looking directly into it was difficult. My shorts flapped painfully against my legs. When I got back I checked with Susan to see if I'd imagined the change, and she said I hadn't.

At about 10 P.M. we started the big Perkins diesel, which hadn't failed us yet. The idea was to warm it up and get it ready to use later, if necessary, to take strain off the anchor rodes by motoring slowly ahead.

As usual, one touch of the starter was enough. The needles jumped in the dials and gradually settled into their accustomed places: temperature 80 degrees centigrade, oil pressure 50 psi, RPM 900, transmission pressure 140 psi, starboard alternator charging at about 20 amps. Under the floorboards, the engine was warm and purring.

When I went down in the cabin to take a leak (the wind was too strong to do it over the side anymore), there was a faint smell of decay. I assumed it was from the garbage bags back on the stern but noticed that instead of getting weaker as I moved forward toward the head, it got stronger. I realized it was coming from two gleaming black-spotted tiger cowrie shells we had found a couple of days earlier, alive, in shallow water just short of the drop-off on the barrier reef. I'd found one and, later, Susan had found the other.

At the time, I hadn't realized that shells in some cultures are considered bad talismans. But when I found my shell, glowing eerily in the darkness of its crevice, I'd felt an odd current that was not the joy of discovery. Still, I hadn't resisted taking it back to the boat and showing it to Susan. As she took its smooth, dark heaviness into her hands she had that same wide-pupiled look she had when we made landfall in Hawaii and dropped anchor here.

We let the animal in my shell gradually die and deliquesce until it could be washed out in salt water. The smell was so horrendous that we tried a different approach when she found hers, boiling it briefly to kill and harden the animal and then picking it out with a fishhook. Her way was more humane and the smell wasn't as bad, but the boiling had caused slight chipping and discoloration.

The two shells were now side by side in a sea-railed pocket on the drop-leaf teak salon table. It was too late to throw them overboard; the animals had already died. They were just beautiful skeletons now, and Susan had always been on good terms with skeletons. She collected bones of all kinds, went out of her way to visit cemeteries, and had once put together a photographic essay on the death markers along the Transpeninsular Highway of Baja California. She'd want to keep hers, and it would be wrong to heave mine even though it was the smellier.

No, the two shells should stay together, in death as in life.

* * *

The boat was beginning to pitch uneasily in the short chop when I came back up to the wheelhouse. Susan, holding on to the grab rails with her small, strong hands, was looking out the window at the one light still visible on shore: the generator-powered electric light in the community center. All the kerosene lanterns were gone now, and the boat could have been floating in outer space. Susan's face was lit from below by the amber numerals on the depth finder, the pale green glow of the GPS, and the lamps in each of the engine dials. Neither of us spoke.

In that same illumination I could see the face of my watch; a little after 11 p.m. We'd been in darkness for five hours and had at least seven more to go before dawn.

Land people, most of them anyway, tend to sleep through the night. It's different on a boat at sea. The watches continue, no matter what time it is. You sleep a few hours at night and a few hours during the day.

In our usual voyaging schedule, the last watch of the night carried over into daylight and Susan took that, while both of mine were in darkness. On long passages I seemed to be awake at night more than during the day, becoming a creature of the night—a small, vulnerable one. I was well acquainted with the stars, the Southern Cross, the moon (in all its phases), the feel but not the look of big ocean swells. It was a fearsome beauty.

Squalls always seemed to come at night. Cold, sharp, horizontally moving raindrops would rattle against the black windows of the wheelhouse, and the sails would begin to boom like shotguns. I'd cut the automatic pilot, trim the sheets, and try to find the wind, which would be shifting wildly through all points of the compass. Confused, choppy seas would broadside the hull, break into the cockpit, and make me worry about the thin glass in the wheelhouse. The seas would be invisible as always, except for the white foam running down their fronts, but they'd sound like sliding rocks.

Ships always passed at night, too, moving at more than 20 knots, so fast they could be on us twenty-five minutes after their lights appeared on the horizon. And once again I'd marvel at how, in the middle of nowhere, two boats on two different courses originating on opposite sides of a vast ocean could pass so terrifyingly close.

I've read a lot of rhapsodies on the joys of night sailing in the trades. Personally, I was always very glad to see the sun come up, to have survived yet another twelve hours of uncertainty, punctuated by not a few of those waking nightmares, snatches of disembodied conversation, lights and huge waves that didn't exist. When dolphins streaked through that darkness like glowing comets, with unearthly breathing and startling churnings and splashes, I'd tell myself they were the spirits of my dead father enjoying themselves and wishing me well on this voyage. But I never believed it.

The sustained force of the wind now seemed over 60 knots, with occasional gusts that felt well over 80. But how could you judge? It was a dark wind, while the storm in Honduras—our only standard of comparison—had been a daytime one. Does being able to see what you're faced with make it worse or better? You'd think better, except that sometimes at sea, when the sun comes up and illuminates the waves you've been taking for granted all night, they look terrifying. All I can say for sure is that this warm, damp, heavy entity sometimes felt a little stronger than anything we'd experienced before, and sometimes quite a bit stronger.

"*Lord Jim,* how are you doing?" asked Wotho Radio. Usually it was the mayor himself who talked to us, but the mayor was away at the President's Invitational Billfishing Tournament at Kwajalein atoll about fifty miles southeast. The speaker's English was better than the acting mayor's, whom we'd met earlier in the day, so we couldn't put a face to the voice. It would have been nice to have been able to. "We're doing okay so far," I said. "Have you heard anything new?"

Nothing new. The storm center was still due sometime after midnight, it was still headed west-northwest, and the present latitude was about 11 degrees. It still should pass well to the north.

"Are you sure you don't want to come ashore?" Wotho Radio asked.

It was the voice of experience talking, and we should have listened. Maybe Susan did listen and wanted to go, but she didn't tell me. I didn't ask her. I couldn't make out her expression in the dim light. I wanted her to stay. I was confident in our technology and even more confident that as long as we stayed together everything would be all right.

We couldn't have rowed ashore, of course. The inflatable dinghy would have been blown downwind like a balloon. But swimming ashore in the warm, cozy water would have been easy. It was only 300 feet to the protected beach. I could have swum in with Susan and then swum back. Or I could have stayed ashore with her and let the *Lord Jim* fend for herself.

"We'll hang on here," I said, trying to make out Susan's face. "But your light is very helpful. It lets us know where we are."

"Okay, roger, roger. Wotho Radio standing by."

The idea of abandoning ship—our home, our career, our life—was unthinkable to me, at least at that point. We weren't in trouble, not even close. There were many things we could do if it got worse, but how much worse could it get? I was prepared to take a chance, and I assumed Susan was too.

I went forward to check the anchors again and, as before, the wind seemed to pick up immediately. I could feel the features on my face changing under it into a wind-tunnel grimace—my lips pulled back over my teeth, my eyes squeezed shut, my cheeks flapping.

I had let out all hundred feet of the nylon rode and needed more, so I tied one of the braided orlon dock lines to it with a double fisherman's bend and fitted another polyethylene chafe guard on the other side of the knot. The wind blew through my fingers and made them clumsy as I paid the line out through the bowsprit roller and snubbed it. On the other bowsprit roller the anchor chain, held with a chain hook attached to a 15-foot length of springy one-inch nylon rope to absorb the jerks, still had some belly left in it.

I was cold and breathless by the time I got back to the wheelhouse. Susan handed me a towel. "It doesn't seem to like me going out there, does it?" I joked. I was always complaining that she took things too personally, even the weather. "That last gust was a good eighty knots, didn't you think?"

She nodded without smiling back.

"Maybe we ought to try putting it in gear," I said. "Take the strain off the lines." My hand was shaking slightly as I pushed the Morse control lever forward and watched the RPMs climb to 1,000, the slowest possible motoring speed. "I'll have to go up again and see what's happening."

She put a warm hand on my arm. "Oh, wear your harness. Please!"

It was the first time she'd sounded fearful; maybe she was wishing she was safely onshore. It should have worried me. "We're at *anchor*, Susan." Grinning. "We're not out in the middle of the ocean. If I fall overboard I can climb back on. Actually, it would be really nice to be in the water." I meant it. The air was filled with cold 80-mph raindrops that stung like buckshot. The water, as I imagined it, would be comforting, almost motherly.

This time there was no question: as soon as I left the wheelhouse the wind gusted to the highest velocity yet. I could tell by the weight of it on my body. I had to crouch and shield my eyes. Through the tears, I could see that the engine had caused us to run up dangerously on the anchor rodes and at the same time fall off to port.

I let the wind carry me back to the wheelhouse and took the engine out of gear. Towel again. "Hope we didn't piss off the storm god," I said, with the old casual reassuring grin. I leaned out the wheelhouse door and shouted, "Sorry! For Christ's sake, we're *s* . . . *o* . . . *o* . . . *o* . . . *o* . . . *r* . . . *r* . . . *y!*"

Maybe if I'd known then what I know now, I wouldn't have shouted so cockily. Maybe. Though the WWVH weather broadcasts told us otherwise, by dusk the storm had actually turned 20 degrees to the southwest and was now headed right at us, with an intensifying wind speed of between 85 and 105 knots.

We were targeted.

The storm god hates technology. For the first time in the four years we'd owned the boat, the depth finder began to malfunction. It would register the correct depth of eighteen feet for a little while, but then the number would be replaced by a line across the screen, meaning that its range had been exceeded or that it was actually sitting on the bottom. The line would be replaced by arbitrary numbers, and then—at increasing intervals—the real ones would come on again. This was unsettling, because a change in depth would be the best way to tell if we were dragging.

Another way would be by the light onshore. But what if the light onshore went out?

A third way could be by means of the GPS, which was accurate to a quarter mile. I programmed a way point that corresponded to the spot where we were anchored so that later, if we seemed to be dragging, we could check our actual position against it.

By this time, Susan had taken up a position on the floor of the wheelhouse near the closed door leading out to the cockpit, the most protected space on board. I was on the settee next to the radio and weatherfax. The boat rolled and pitched sharply, and the noises around us had deepened in tone from a screaming to a deep thrumming vibration. Talk was difficult; there didn't seem to be much to say anyway. The wind outside blew our thoughts away, even though inside the air was calm.

I wondered idly whether the large wheelhouse windows would blow in. The big diesel pulsed. We hung on and waited for the clock to move, and it had never moved more slowly.

Sometime after midnight, I saw that the light onshore was no longer there, although I thought I could still see the loom of the island. There was a chance we could be dragging.

"I better go check the anchors again," I said.

"*Oh, God, don't go out there.*"

I grinned and said something flip, even though I understood very well what she was worried about. To go out would make the storm worse. At the time, I didn't wonder how bad things would have to get before the insouciance she hated so much gave way to tenderness and sympathy.

I tugged the wheelhouse door open. "Well, anyway, the garbage is still on board."

Susan didn't answer. I turned to see why not (in the darkness I couldn't make out her expression), almost went back, almost put my arms around her, but instead I went out and closed the door behind me.

Standing upright on deck now was impossible, so I hauled myself forward from handhold to handhold in the crouch of a man who has had too much to drink—the old Hurricane Walk.

The anchors were holding, but the nylon rode was tight as a piano string and the thick nylon spring line on the anchor chain was stretching more than a foot with every heave of the boat. As it stretched, it chafed against the sharp edge of the bulwark next to the bowsprit. The belly in the chain was gone.

I considered letting out more chain but that would have meant a complicated series of maneuvers. Susan would have to add power from the engine to take the strain off the rodes. When the strain was off, I'd have to reach down with my hand and release the steel bar that locked into the cogs of the windlass and held it immovable.

As Susan cut back the power and the chain paid out, I'd have to control it with the windlass brake while slacking the nylon rode with my other hand. When they were both out enough, I'd have to snub them (the chain with the windlass brake and the nylon with the cleat) and attach the chain hook again. If the brake slipped while I was releasing or engaging the locking bar and the strain of the boat suddenly came back on the chain, I could easily lose a finger or a hand.

I decided not to try, to wait it out and hope for the best. How much worse could it get? We had a third 45-pound CQR plow anchor to throw in an emergency. But for the first time, I began to feel a hint of passivity, a slight inclination to say to myself, "It's gone too far; it's out of my hands."

Back in the cockpit, I saw that our ten-foot inflatable dinghy, which had served us faithfully and well since we'd bought the boat, was floating upside down behind us. As I watched, the wind blew it right side up again; then for a while it left the water completely and streamed out behind us at the end of its painter like a kite. I grabbed the line and shortened it up until the dinghy was snubbed against the hull, but the chafing was worse that way. I tried to haul the whole thing into the cockpit but didn't have the strength.

Finally, I just let it go, feeling that curious passivity gain a little. And, thinking about it later, I realized that the garbage must have blown away by then or it would have been in my way.

For the first time, Susan and I didn't talk about whether the wind had picked up while I was outside. "I don't think the spring line is going to hold much longer," I said, as she handed me the towel, pushing it into my hand as she'd been trained to pass a scalpel to a surgeon in an operating theater. When I tried to check our position against the way point I'd programmed into the GPS, I noticed some unfamiliar symbols next to the numerals. The numerals didn't change when I punched the keys, they didn't respond. There was some malfunction in it, too.

Normally, I would have opened the chart table, taken out the GPS manual, and painstakingly gone through it to find out what the numerals signified. But I didn't. I just didn't seem to have it in me. I sat down on the settee to rest for a minute, and the feeling of inertia gained another notch.

Susan was back in her protected position by the wheelhouse door, staring at me. We were witnessing a performance. What next? Nothing we had been through before in our lives had prepared us for this, but we stayed calm because we had each other. Because everything was going to work out. And because at that moment there was nothing else to do.

Except jump overboard and swim for shore. It would have been easy. But even now, I was pretty sure that the wind wasn't going to get much stronger, that if the spring line broke the chain would hold, that if the chain broke, the emergency anchor on another 200-foot three-quarter–inch nylon rode could replace it. If it didn't we could beach the boat under power, make her fast to some palm trees, and repair the damage when the storm had passed. The big propeller gave so much thrust I still didn't want to put it in gear and risk overriding the rodes.

"Jesus," Susan said, as a banshee gust once again stretched the limits of what we could imagine. Her eyes looked black. There was a heavy, dense thud and the hull lurched backward off the wind for an instant and came up again. "There goes the spring line," I said, on my way out the door. Up on the bow, the anchor chain was rigid as a steel rod. The lunatic wind blew my brain clean. There was nothing to do but let the force carry me back to the cockpit.

My head stayed empty—*too empty to put the engine in gear*—as we sat in the wheelhouse and waited for the chain to break. Or not. The passive feeling gained a few more notches. Five or ten minutes later the chain did break, with the same dense thud. The hull lurched backward again but did not seem to bring up.

Blessed action. The tonic of movement, of carrying out a plan. Susan was at the wheel, applying enough power to move the boat up parallel to the anchor we were still attached to. I was out on the foredeck again, struggling with the emergency anchor. The plan was: when we got into position I'd drop it, and we'd fall back again on the two rodes. I waved my arm, motioning her forward, but the boat had turned far enough broadside to the wind for the high deckhouse to catch its full force. We were blown over at a 45-degree angle and held there, as if the 8,800 pounds of ballast in the keel didn't exist.

* * *

We had entered the realm of the storm god. The performance had turned into a demonstration. We were his, now. He set the rules. He made the plans. He wrote the script.

Up on the bow, though, I was so busy reacting that I didn't have time to think. Everything seemed as natural as anything else, as in a dream.

The heavy anchor, the coil of rode, and I slid down the steeply inclined deck to leeward and brought up against the bulwark. I worked slowly and methodically to get things cleared away; the hull now broke the wind so I felt comfortable, as if I could work there forever.

Reality now being beyond question, it didn't surprise me in the least that our little waterproof flashlight, which I'd used on all previous ventures forward, was dimming out. And neither did it come as a great shock, when I finally got the anchor over the side and began to pay out the rode, that there was no strain at the other end. It wasn't holding.

Neither was there much strain on the other rode, when I tested it. Maybe we were still drifting down on it, after having powered upwind to drop the emergency.

Anyway, the job was done. When I stood up to work my way aft, the wind caught me and for a second I was flying. I landed on my knees on our newly nonskidded deck and skidded over the sharp little nubbles, pushed by solid air, wondering how much skin and flesh would be left but, clambering into the tilted cockpit, too busy to look.

"Head her up in the wind!" I yelled at Susan. She was clinging to the wheel to stop herself from slipping down the floor. I closed the wheelhouse door and latched it, and suddenly the enveloping nightmare outside turned stagy and unreal, like a movie from the thirties. I felt her warm, dry body against me as I turned the wheel into the wind and applied power.

We couldn't hear the engine but the tachometer registered 2,200 RPM, full power. It made no difference at all. The boat stayed broadside to the wind, held by it at 45 degrees from the vertical and drifting to leeward, not moving forward or heading up. The depth finder continued to malfunction, but I knew there were coral heads near us and expected one or both of the anchors to snag and pull the bow around. We had shipped no water, and once the bow was back in the wind the boat could straighten up again.

It was as if the anchors didn't exist. We continued to drift to leeward, and now I noticed the engine temperature was into the danger zone, well over boiling. No surprise: it was all part of what was happening. I shut it down, rather than run the risk of ruining it forever; both the propeller and the cooling system intake must have been out of the water.

My watch read 1:10 a.m. I noticed the clasp had been damaged as I'd wrestled with the anchor, so I took it off and carefully put it next to my glasses on the ledge under the wheelhouse windows. It was an old Rolex Oyster diving watch my father had given me when I was eighteen, and I didn't want to lose it. "Well," I said to Susan, "you

better call Wotho on the radio and tell them we're drifting"—I checked the compass—"south, out of control."

She called, but (no surprise) there was no answer. Then
she said, "Do you think we better get our life jackets on?"

I shrugged and grinned, a strange reflex, but there it
was. I'd done all I could. Life jackets were her area of responsibility, her decision. To me they'd always been a little
like the EPIRB: a harbinger, a Jonah. An admission of defeat.

"Well, do you?" She sounded angry.

"I guess we should," I said.

The life jackets were inflatable Mae West–type
U-shaped vests. You put your head through the upside-
down U. The two ends of it were attached to a web belt
that you fastened around your waist with a jam buckle. You
inflated it by blowing into a tube past a one-way valve. We
put them on and stood there on the tilted wheelhouse floor,
looking at each other. If anything, seeing Susan in the jacket
made things even less real than before.

"I guess we shouldn't blow them up completely right
now," I said. "We need to be able to maneuver."

She put her mouth to the tube and blew hers up about
two-thirds of the way. When I tried to blow mine up,
nothing happened. "Do you have to twist it or something?"
I asked. "No air is going in."

"No you don't have to twist it," she said impatiently.
"Just blow."

I blew as hard as I could, felt the one-way valve give
reluctantly and the vest inflate. I stopped when it was one-
third full.

We drifted downwind in silence for a while. Inside the wheelhouse it was still warm and dry. Someone in Kwajalein was speaking English on the radio, about supplies he'd be delivering somewhere the next day. His call sign was "Mr. Bill."

"Sooner or later we're going to hit the reef," I said. "Or an island. I don't know how much time we have, but we've got to think about what we're going to need." My mind felt sluggish. We both seemed slow, in movement and thought, as if we were in a dream.

Gradually we assembled the emergency items that Susan had prepared: a grab bag of flares, another flashlight, a pocket knife, a compass, a signal mirror, a large polyethylene waterproof container with a first-aid kit and drugs, emergency rations, fishing line and hooks, ship's and personal papers, my swim fins, the EPIRB.

"You better put your watch and glasses in the waterproof container," Susan said.

It was an impressive, foresighted idea, but I never got around to implementing it. I was trying to coax my sluggish mind to think of more immediate things we'd need. *Wet suits?* We each had a three-millimeter-thick full-body surfing wet suit that would help buoy us up, protect us from the coral, and keep us warm, but they were in the forepeak locker, and the forepeak was full of stuff from on deck. I started down to get them anyway but Susan begged me not to. She was worried about a propane gas explosion, and indeed the red light of the gas sensor had been on for some time. But more than anything, anything in the world at that moment, she didn't want me to leave her alone.

Looking around the wheelhouse and the cockpit for more accessible things, I noticed the pile of dock lines formerly hidden by the bags of garbage. I selected a fifteen-foot three-quarter-inch line and tied the ends around our waists, using bowlines, a knot that doesn't slip tighter or jam. "Now you don't have to worry," I said. "I'll never leave you." I do believe I was grinning when I said it. "Is it tight enough?"

She pulled at it. "I don't think so."

I undid it and tied it again. I didn't want it too tight in case it snagged on something and she needed to get out of it. "How's that?"

She raised her eyes, looked me full in the face for a full count of five (I remember every count), and nodded.

We finally grounded with the kind of jarring lurch that usually makes a sailor's heart dive overboard, but all I felt was a strange relief. "Well, there's the reef." I nodded wisely. At last something had happened the way we'd thought it would.

The wheelhouse was still warm and cozy. Electronic equipment glowed blue, green, amber, and red. The radio crackled with snatches of talk. And the quarter-inch safety-glass windows still safely sealed us in.

Our keel bounced at shorter and shorter intervals but never completely settled, as the surf picked it up and dropped it over and over again on the coral. I turned on the roof-mounted searchlight and spun it around, looking for land. There was nothing in sight but howling, undifferentiated blackness. The light made it worse.

Eventually, we slid open the heavy teak wheelhouse door and worked our way out into the real world. We were still removed, not really with it, like newborn babies. The tilted hull rose over our heads and broke the unimaginable force of the wind. To leeward a strange white element that was a mixture of water, air, and rocks hissed and rushed. Invisible surf from the lagoon pounded the exposed bottom of the hull at our backs while unseen waves coming across the reef from the open ocean occasionally broke directly into the cockpit and threw us around. There was one thing, though, that we knew for sure. The water was warmer than the air.

Side by side, clutching the things we'd gathered together, we sat on the uptilted cockpit thwart, our feet braced on the downtilted one. All the literature said to stick with the boat until the last minute. There was no question of inflating the life raft—it would have vanished immediately. Our best chance was that the hull might work its way higher and higher onto the shallow reef until it was solid. Meanwhile, the searchlight continued to play on nothingness, unless you called that white firehosing element rushing at the leeward edge of the cockpit something.

The boat was already breaking up. When I went into the wheelhouse to look for the diving knife (still connected by our fifteen-foot rope) I saw the leeward windows, closest to the elements, had shattered. The teakwood components of the wheelhouse had started to split off jaggedly from the fiberglass of the hull. Down in the cabin, the red warning light of the propane gas sensor pulsed. Water, mixed no doubt with acid from our new Surrette Type D batteries, was over a corner of the floorboards and climbing up the settee toward our new blue canvas seat covers.

The knife was nowhere to be found. I reeled myself back along the rope to the small wet person alone in the cockpit, sat down next to her again, and put my arm around her. Automatically she leaned forward to clear her hair. She always did that, because she hated to have it pulled.

The last wave held us underwater for too long. It was time to go, and quite easy. We let the soft, almost blood-temperature element carry us clear of the foundering hull.

We were holding hands. The searchlight, now only a few feet up, shone away from us into blackness. The wind was easier, with only our heads in it. The noise was somewhere in the background. We were breathing the element, and it seemed breathable.

Drifting downwind from the hull, Susan's voice came more like a thought. "Where are we?"

I heard my matter-of-fact answer. "I don't know." The searchlight was extinguished, leaving us in darkness. The boat was gone. I blew on the tube to inflate my vest the rest of the way but no air would go in. A wave from the lagoon broke over us, tearing her hand out of mine, scraping my back against the reef. It was not sharp coral here, but weed-covered smooth rock. That was lucky.

Three-foot waves began breaking over us about every fifteen seconds. In the darkness we couldn't see them coming. They were big enough to roll us over and disorient us, to hold us underwater for a few seconds, to scrape us against the rocks but not to smash us. I held Susan around the waist with one arm and with the other held on to my partially inflated life vest.

Its belt had come undone and the U-shaped part had slipped off my head. In the darkness, I couldn't make out how to put it back on. The valve was still stuck. All the things we had brought with us had disappeared by this time, or I would have put on my fins. They would have made swimming twice as easy.

In some of the waves we couldn't hold on to each other. We'd catch our breath, get oriented, get a new grip. Another wave would come and go. We'd start the process over. Then I lost contact with Susan completely. I pulled on the rope. There was no resistance; finally I felt the knot at my fingertips, the empty loop. Nothing was visible.

The energy I used up in the next three or four strokes equaled all the previous energy combined. But she was there, not far away. Quite near. My arm was back around her soft waist and her voice was back inside my head, almost like a thought. "I've come out of my jacket."

She was holding on to it now, like I was holding on to mine. Her wet round head, mouth open and facing up, was in silhouette—against what? Against blackness, and yet I could see it clearly, the first thing I'd been able to see since we'd left the boat. Between waves, I tried to fit the loop back over her shoulders, under her arms. And failed.

We were in deeper water, no more rocks under our feet. Had we drifted out over the reef into the open ocean? Her voice again. *"Hold me up."* An arm around my neck, a hug, an embrace, like so many times before.

"Not the neck, pet. Not the neck." Obediently, she took her arm away. Her back was to me, my arm was around her waist. A few more waves rolled through and I yelled, "Hold on to your jacket. Hold on to the rope. Are you all right? You have to tell me if you're not all right."

She was making an oddly reassuring noise, *"Oh, oh, oh, oh."* I knew it well. It was the noise she made when she was scared—as we rowed our tiny inflatable dinghy closer and closer to a sleeping whale or when a car shot out in front of us on the highway without warning. When she made that noise, I knew, there wasn't any real danger. When the danger was real—when our car actually left the road on a rainy, foggy night in upstate New York and flew through the air into a ten-foot-deep culvert; when the seventy-foot shrimp boat broke loose in the last storm in Honduras and began to drift down on us; when the Cessna 172 I was trying to land began to porpoise down the runway—there had been no noise from her at all.

I knew how she hated and feared being rolled in the waves even on a good day, but as long as she made that noise there couldn't be any problem. Things would work out. We were together.

We were underwater again. I opened my eyes and saw her clearly, as if she were outlined in black fire. She was relaxed. There was a little smile on her lips and her eyes were half closed. Her long hair spread out in the water. The top of her head was about a foot under the surface, and when I put my hand under her chin and tried to push up, another wave was there.

She moved farther away from me below the surface and the black light around her was extinguished. I reached out and felt her hair—the soft, fine ends. The tips of my fingers could still feel it as the tickly bubbles and warm currents of the next wave curled around me, wrapped me up, and did what they wanted with me.

I can feel it now.

The Voice

The voice started talking in the womblike dark water sometime after I lost Susan. I was dog-paddling with one hand, holding the limp life vest with the other. I seemed to be in the open ocean now, with infinity in all directions, but whether or not I was on the surface was unclear. I could feel myself breathing something—air, water, or both. The storm seemed vague. *You blew it,* the voice said, and I felt myself crying, but it didn't seem to matter very much. *She's gone.* I would soon be gone myself. Maybe I already was gone. Is this what drowning feels like?

If it is, then drowning is mostly a process of waiting. Waiting for it all to be over with and wondering every once in a while how you'd know. No revelations, no home movies of your life, no regrets. No strong concerns, either about Susan or myself. A lonely way to die, but then what isn't? "What is the answer?" Gertrude Stein was asked as she slipped away, and she answered, "What is the question?" Neither the voice nor the womblike element that I floated in offered anything profound. I did have a feeling, though, that when I died I'd be able to see again.

Our story was almost complete. It was going to have an honorable end—and in a way, a happy one. We weren't going to die in each other's arms, but we were going to die in the same storm, in the same element, probably just about at the same time. Death was not going to put us asunder, the storm had done that; it was going to join us together again for good.

So the feel of sand under my slowly kicking feet was out of place, unbelievable. Sand instead of coral could mean a beach. A beach could mean an island. The story was being botched, I felt dimly, but there was nothing I could do about it; when I lost Susan I lost all control. My body wanted to survive, and each time my toes touched the sand I felt them dig in and push as hard as they could. They touched more and more often—they knew what they were doing.

I knew I was on land when I felt myself leave the water on hands and knees, felt the screaming air sandpaper my body raw, felt my arms and legs move me up, over a small ledge and partially out of the blast. The land was shaking. The air boomed. I pulled my knees up to my chin, wrapped my arms around my head, and lay there. *So you made it,* the voice said. *Nice going.*

Someone was laughing, a booming, roaring, awful laugh. I burrowed into the dense, thorny brush in front of me until I was too tired to move.

Sometime in the darkness the eye of the storm passed through, and in the half hour or so of calm I stumbled along the invisible beach calling for her until the wind screamed me down. Coming in from the southeast instead of the northwest, it seemed if anything stronger than before. The island vibrated in a deep base register, and big heavy things seemed to be flying over my head and into the water.

At first light, I began searching the parts of the beach that were protected enough to stand on (the wind had dropped a little from its full force). Now I could see, though fuzzily without my glasses, where everything had happened. I had washed ashore at the northern end of a long, thin, low island, part of the uninhabited chain that encircled Wotho lagoon. A spit of sand led out into open water, a kind of channel in the reef with large, curling brown waves indicating a fair depth and current. Barely visible through the rain, blown sand, spume, and the blur of nearsightedness was a small rock ledge a few hundred yards away on the other side of the channel.

The *Lord Jim* must have hit near the rocky ledge. After we abandoned her, we'd been swept into the rough channel. There was no sign of the boat. Everything was brownish-whitish-gray, the color of the wind blowing the tops off the dirty waves and mixing them with air. The things that had been roaring through the air over my head were the tops of palm trees. They were in the surf, washing up and down the beach along with other detritus. *How do you like it now, gentlemen?* the voice asked.

Each time I searched the beach, a figure was there, cottony and vague, like everything else appeared without my glasses. The first few times I ran toward it, fearing I'd die before I got there. It would recede ahead of me, fade out, or turn into something else. But even when I couldn't see it, I felt it was there. I began to dread it, but desperately needed it at the same time.

I couldn't imagine Susan herself—where she might be if she wasn't on that beach. What she was thinking? It came to me later, as if transmitted by some celestial EPIRB: *Where is he? God, where did he go?*

I lost count of how many times I walked the two miles of coastline, searched through the high mounds of debris and dense thickets all the way to the other side, but the last few times there was nothing new, nothing more to come ashore. The narrative of shipwreck was starkly told by what was there, almost everything from the boat that wasn't bolted on and some things that were.

Nothing of Susan's was on the beach but—as if she'd arranged it before departing—I quickly and easily found all the things I needed to survive. There was the waterproof emergency container, which would have had my glasses and watch in it if I'd listened to her, but which did have the other things she'd stocked it with: beef jerky for protein and gumballs for quick energy, various antibiotic and pain pills for the coral cuts on my feet and legs; the ship's papers and our passports, which the authorities would need when I reported what had happened. There was her precious Class I EPIRB, still blinking away and transmitting its special coded message via satellite to the nearest U.S. Coast Guard station— probably Honolulu, more than two thousand miles to the northeast. Scattered up and down were most of the foam rubber cushions in their new canvas covers. I could lie on the foam and zip myself up in a cover like a sleeping bag for protection from the rain. And completely buried in sand except for one arm was my black full-body wet suit.

I uncovered it gently, and as I did so suddenly I was back in the boat's wheelhouse, drifting downwind out of control, about to go down to the forepeak and get our wet suits and hearing her say, "No. Please don't leave me."

But this time I did go down. I got the wet suits and we put them on in the wheelhouse. Their buoyancy kept us afloat after we'd abandoned ship, and the three-millimeter foam protected us nicely from the coral and kept us warm both in the water and after we'd crawled out on the beach and under the bushes. They were what saved us.

The scene had the reality of a drug hallucination. It was to be the first of many replays, each with its own new twist and each having a happy ending. They're still happening.

Tough Questions

Two days after the typhoon, the villagers of Wotho stood clustered on the beach watching a figure walk toward them out of the spume and haze to the southeast. The sky was full of fast-moving broken clouds, through which the sun appeared and disappeared in a kind of celestial stuttering. The water in the lagoon now was milky blue instead of brown, full of detritus and still choppy, with good-sized breakers pounding the sand. The more adventurous boys were running down the wet sand as the water pulled back, waiting until the last moment for the next wave to break, then scattering back up the beach ahead of the spray like sandpipers. In back of the beach, among fallen palms, stripped breadfruit trees, and a few huge old naked banyans, the village of Wotho no longer existed.

I'd left the island I'd washed ashore on at dawn of the second day, when the tide was dead low and the top of the reef was only a few feet underwater. The surge in the deep channel north of the sand spit had subsided enough for me to swim. Wotho Island, I knew, was somewhere out of sight to the north, four or five islands away. There would be other channels to swim between the islands.

I was missing most of the skin from my right knee where it had scraped along the deck, there was a deep coral cut in my right ankle, and the bottoms of both feet were crisscrossed with slashes from walking on sharp rocks and thorny brush, but the salt water had kept them clean and as yet I felt no pain. My body seemed numb, as numb as my mind, with just that insistent voice between me and silence. If I didn't make it, I wouldn't have to listen anymore.

The voice now was dispensing ironic platitudes and inanities like *Every cloud has a silver lining.* Or *Raindrops keep falling on my head.* Or it would tender a running commentary on whatever I happened to be doing: *Set up something to catch the rainwater, you idiot!* It had said hateful things, but this babbling was worse.

As I got closer, the boys stopped playing in the waves and joined the rest of the crowd. There were maybe thirty people standing there silently. I was carrying my wet suit over my arm and wearing just the shorts I'd washed ashore in. I wondered how I looked to them.

Nobody screamed and ran. Nobody welcomed me either. They looked receptive mainly, shyly waiting for me to make the first move, and I remembered that almost none of them spoke English.

At last an old man pushed his way through, walked up to me with a big grin, and shook my hand.

I took a deep breath and stared at him.

"Thanks to God," he said. "You both okay."

I felt my head turn from side to side. "Oh, I so sorry," he said, although the smile lingered on his face as if he didn't believe me.

I realized we'd met him the morning before the storm. He'd been one of a group standing around the community center while Susan and I had argued about whether or not to lend the village our only large-scale chart of the area. Susan was wearing a pair of faded brown hiking shorts, a lavender long-sleeved shirt, and a tooled Mexican leather belt I'd given her for Christmas. The Cartier mood ring had been on the ring finger of her left hand. She'd just washed her long bleached hair, and before she had we'd argued about that, too, because we were running out of time. Still, she'd wanted to look her best.

The acting mayor had looked worried. They had a radio but had been getting no reports. I'd shown them a weatherfax we'd received on our new machine and we'd gone to the dispensary where their radio was so I could show them the right frequency for the hourly reports from Hawaii. The trouble was, they had no idea about latitude and longitude, which oriented all the reports.

"You better go back to the boat and get them our chart," Susan had said.

"We don't have time, for God's sake," I'd said. "And besides, we need our chart."

We'd stood there staring at each other. Her face had been pale and her eyes steady. It reminded me of the way she'd looked at the airport owner after our close shave in the Cessna.

Before our time together, I never would have gotten the chart. I would have felt fine about not getting it: the villagers were going to be safe on land while we'd be taking our chances out in the boat. Now, even with the storm coming, I felt myself blushing with embarrassment.

Susan said she'd wait on shore while I rowed out for the chart so the dinghy would be lighter. I launched it and began to pull away, facing her. She was standing in a clearing next to the white wooden church with the wind blowing her hair and her lavender shirt nicely set off by the light green of the blowing palm leaves. She was surrounded two deep by a group of laughing girls, teaching them a new phrase in English that I could just hear from the dinghy: "So long, see you tomorrow."

The girls laughed as they repeated it, and Susan looked up and waved at me. Her smile seemed strangely luminous. I heard a click in my mind; if I'd had the camera I would have photographed her. As it turned out, though, I didn't need the camera. The image is still as clear as if I'd just seen it.

The acting mayor, a short, powerfully built man with deep wrinkles of responsibility on his forehead, was waiting when I arrived at the village (followed by about half the group from the beach). I tried to prepare for questions, but he was either too busy or too embarrassed to ask any. For a second, I thought he didn't know, but then he said the U.S. Coast Guard in Honolulu needed to talk to me on the radio. So the EPIRB she'd been so proud of had worked.

The community center was filled from wall to wall with women and kids nursing, cooking, gossiping. The elderly radio operator looked like John Huston, the same kind of quizzical foxiness and gat teeth. No one looked unhappy or particularly surprised to see me. The woman who had given us fritters the morning before the storm gave me one now, with just about the same smile. It was an admirable, practical way of dealing with disaster, but it made me want to scream.

Almost immediately I was connected to Lieutenant Steve Sebelico, at the Coast Guard's Joint Rescue Control Center. He sounded very young and kept saying, "I know you've been through a lot, but just try to hold on for a little while longer. You're doing great so far, just great."

No problem. His voice seemed full of sympathy and he avoided the tough questions, either out of delicacy or because they didn't matter. Telling him what had happened was like confession.

I told him I wanted to tell the family myself, before they heard it from anyone else. "Please," I said. "Do you understand how important it is? Do you?" It was a startling discovery, after all, to find the thing I'd dreaded most was in fact the thing I couldn't live without.

Lieutenant Sebelico said he did, now sounding (was it my imagination?) a little paternal. He said a Coast Guard plane from Kwajalein would be out the next day to do an air search of the area, but he was relying on me for "ground support." I told him I'd search as many of the islands as I could get to in the village's little outboard.

The first call I made was to Ashley in Washington. "Just the machine, sir," the Coast Guard operator said in a flat voice. Reflexively, I prepared to leave a message, but luckily he'd already disconnected. Machines answered at Page's in Rhode Island, Susan's sister's, and her two brothers'.

The only person I reached was her mother, Julia. She had already heard. I found out later that Susan's sister, Mary, had been on hold to Lieutenant Sebelico while he talked to me, and that as soon as we'd finished he had—dryly and in clinical detail—given her the full report. They had known something was wrong since the first EPIRB signal, about nine in the morning their time two days before. "I just don't know what to say to you, Gordon," Julia said coolly.

I called my daughter Diana, who was crying and asked how I was.

"I'm fine," I said, shocked, almost in outrage. "I'm perfectly all right. Don't worry about me."

Dusk was falling by the time I finished the last radio call. I poured a bucket of fresh water from a cistern over my body, ate my allotted share of the village's last pot of pork and rice, and was shown to a kind of shelf in the community center to sleep on. Children were talking and giggling all around me, climbing over me, touching me, and I found the contact comforting. The board I was lying on seemed oddly soft, at least at first.

Sometime during the night, the acting mayor cleared a place among the children and lay down next to me. It was as if we were two children ourselves, safe and dry. He lay on his stomach; I learned over the course of the night that this is the most comfortable way to lie on a board.

"All right now?" he said, in the kind of low voice a child will use talking to another child in the next bed, in the dark.

"Yes. I'm glad to be here."

"Not hungry?"

"No, no. Plenty of food, thank you."

He sighed and didn't say anything for a while, but I could feel the questions inside him.

Finally he asked the toughest. "So how you make it?"

"I just kept swimming," I said. "Until I washed ashore."

"You swim good, hah?"

"Yes."

"She no?"

"Not as good," I said.

"You strong man," he said, as if he understood now.

"I was trying to hold her," I said. "But the waves were too strong. We came out of our life jackets. Then I lost her."

He didn't say anything.

"It was dark," I said. "I couldn't find her again. We had no lights."

Silence.

"She went down. *She was underneath the water.* I didn't know where she was."

He cleared his throat and seemed to hum a snatch of tune. Then he didn't say anything for a long time. I thought he'd gone to sleep. Finally, though, he asked another question. "Before. Why you no sail away?"

I could feel my heart beating against the board. "We should have," I said. "There are a lot of things we should have done."

DONE WITH
THE COMPASS

❡ ❡ ❡

Thanksgiving

At the end of the long metal tube leading from the airplane to the gate at Logan Airport in Boston, I could fuzzily make out two tall, thin, handsome young women. They were waving madly. One was carrying a big-eyed blond child, and as I came closer I could see both women were crying. I almost looked behind me to see who they were waving at, although of course I knew they were my daughters. Even without my glasses.

I'd last seen them a little more than two months ago, but now they looked shockingly adult. How old were they,

exactly? Their scented hair against my face, their comforting arms around me, their loving voices. They were twenty-
five and twenty-three, grown up indeed. And how old did
that make me?

"Are you all right, Grampa? Do you have any cuts?"

Grampa! I told my four-year-old grandson, Avery,
about the infected ankle and the abraded knee—the reason I was limping—and for the first time I accepted his name
for me. "You're so brave, Grampa," he said, shaking his
curls.

Avery's eyes were wide, innocent, admiring. I could
hardly look at him. *You're so brave.* It must be what he'd
considerately been told to say, or maybe he'd thought it
up himself and was young enough to believe it.

Susan wasn't there. Her absence filled the Volvo station wagon as we drove away from the airport through the
Callahan Tunnel under Boston Harbor and up onto the
freeway. This Thanksgiving being the most ironic day of
my life, it wasn't surprising that Susan's absence brought
my daughters and me closer together than any time since
I'd left them to go with her.

I asked them where I'd be staying. On the phone
during a stopover in Honolulu, my cousin had told me
they'd decided to put me up in a hotel, even though my
ex-wife had offered the guest room in her family's house
in the suburb of Weston. Diana and Avery were living there
with Holly, her new husband, Dick, and her eighty-eight-
year-old mother. Four generations of proper Bostonians.

It had occurred to me that Susan would want me to

stay with her family, but they hadn't invited me. I had no money or credit cards, nothing except my passport and the ship's papers, which Susan had stored in the waterproof container. I had no clothes except a pair of pants and a shirt given me by the minister in Wotho, a jersey, and a pair of canvas beach shoes I'd bought in the Marshall Islands airport. Diana, suddenly an engine of efficiency, had been arranging everything. I felt volitionless, as I had increasingly since the storm, but now I took comfort in it.

"Weston's fine," Diana said. "Everything's okay."

"They put the turkey in this morning," Avery said. "Mmmmm. And they're baking pies." Avery was on a macrobiotic diet, like his mother, and Thanksgiving was his one chance to howl.

"Are you sure it's okay?"

"It's fine," Julie said.

"What did Holly say?"

Julie looked uncomfortable. "Well, when we heard the news some people were pretty upset with you. But it's all right now. Really. They'll be disappointed if you don't come."

My sister, Susie, said to my cousin, when he told her the news, "He has a lot of explaining to do." She didn't fly back from California for the service, in fact flew the opposite direction, to the Far East, putting the world between us. She announced her intention of splitting the family trust. "I'm scared of you, Gordon," she told me, in a phone conversation from Perth, Australia.

The wife of a close friend from my days as a journalist was sure that I'd saved the manuscript of a novel-in-progress from the wreck even as I'd failed to save Susan.

But at that moment, I couldn't think beyond Ashley and Page. They were celebrating Thanksgiving with their father and stepmother in Rhode Island, but soon I'd be trying to tell them exactly how everything had happened. Nothing I might say would change the fact that I was standing in front of them alive.

Over the thirteen years of our marriage, Holly and I had put in a lot of time at her family's old wooden house in Weston. I'd courted her there; it had been a safe haven between jobs. The sight of it made me realize how exhausted I was. "Can you get me upstairs without anyone seeing me?" I asked Diana. "And then tell me when it's time to eat?" She did it adroitly, through a side door. The house smelled of turkey.

I lay down on the bed in the familiar guest room where Holly and I had spent many a night, in the old days, and listened to the family prepare the Thanksgiving meal down below. Time had gone funny; everything could have been happening twenty years ago. There was the same musty smell in the room, the same battered, uncomfortable, semiantique furniture, the same dim November light (we'd always seemed to end up in Boston in November) through the window. Even my former in-laws' voices, coming not so faintly up the stairs, were the same.

Twenty years ago Susan was in my future, instead of in my past. In the best of all possible presents we'd be having Thanksgiving in Ponape, in the Caroline Islands, celebrating our escape from Typhoon Gay.

Somehow, it had happened otherwise. Holly is an astrologer. She'd be glad to tell me how everything is written in the stars.

Lying down was better than standing up, pondering time was better than talking, sleeping would have been best of all, but I was under no illusion about getting any. The only real sleep I'd had since the storm had been aboard the old LST landing craft that brought relief supplies to Wotho from Kwajalein. The captain, a huge Fijian named Moses ("Just remember the Ten Commandments") Cama, had lent me his tender and a crewman and maneuvered his ship to help me conduct a search of all the islands in the atoll I hadn't been able to get to in the village's smaller outboard. Even the *Lord Jim*'s hull had vanished without a trace.

We left Wotho forever at sundown, me in tears and he circling the last tiny islet, blowing his horn to catch Susan's attention, until I told him it was no use. After a seaman's meal of fish and rice, I fell into a berth and slept until morning. It was the familiar roll of the ocean that let me.

A soft, shy knock on the door. It opened a crack to show a sky-blue eye three feet above the ground. "We're about to start . . . Gordon," Avery whispered, and came into the room, staring at me in wonder. "Can I see your cuts?"

He'd been briefed again. "It's all right," I told him, rolling up my pants leg. "You can call me Grampa if you want."

My twenty or so ex-relations were seated at the large dining room table around platters of winter squash and green beans, cranberry and mint sauce, gravy and giblets. Two turkeys were steaming on the sideboard. There was an empty seat between Diana and Julie, and I made for it.

Ah, Boston. Where else could you come back after adultery, divorce, shipwreck, and tragedy halfway around the world and be treated as if you'd never left? As if twenty years had never passed? The pale Waspy faces around the table were different—the older people were now my contemporaries, my generation—but the atmosphere was the same. Polite talk about practical things like septic tanks, cellar seepage, plowing driveways. Old tweed jackets and baggy-seated khaki pants for the men, full-skirted, highnecked, long-sleeved dim wool dresses for the ladies (except for my daughters, who were wearing black sheaths). Anyway, we greeted each other naturally—or unnaturally, depending on your perspective.

"How's your Uncle Cummins?" my eighty-eight-year-old ex-mother-in-law called from the head of the table. My uncle had impressed her at our wedding twenty-six years ago as being a member in good standing of "polite" Philadelphia. "Very well, thank you," I answered, in spite of the fact that my uncle was now deceased. It didn't matter anyway. She was only acknowledging what my uncle represented.

There was only one reference to what had happened, by an Irish ex-brother-in-law. He called it "my problem," as in "Hope your problem comes out all right." As for the rest, there's something to be said for the stiff upper lip. If it's stiff enough you can almost convince yourself that, whatever happens, life goes on exactly as before.

After the feast, in the early darkness of Boston November, my daughters drove me to Beacon Hill, where Susan's family had gathered for their Thanksgiving. They were Bostonians too, but grew up less concerned with being proper than with their father's terrible illness. They lived controlled lives with an underlay of fine zaniness. In their spare time they wrote comic novels, children's books, songs. They made family movies and, as children, invented an entire civilization and language of their own.

Susan's mother hadn't mellowed with age at all. She was stout and loud, gat-toothed, fiercely feminist since divorcing her husband, and had just won a bout with the cancer that would eventually kill her. After I sent her a contrary book called *Difficult Women*, profiles of Germaine Greer, Jean Rhys, and Sonia Orwell among others, I could do no wrong. Until I made the mistake of sending her *The Bridges of Madison County*.

Susan and her mother, two strong-willed, independent women, had their ups and downs. Before we'd left for Micronesia they were debating in terse letters the value of seeing a therapist together. In their ups, they'd take long walks, visit museums, play Scrabble into the wee hours, discuss books, gossip about friends and family, and agree on many of the same issues they fought over in their downs.

Susan's mother lived in the first-floor apartment of her youngest son Ned's town house, where the family had gathered and where she'd first heard the news. Ned wrote me about it later:

> For us, Susan died when we sat down with my mother. She knew it was something bad because all of her children were there. We said: "We have something to tell you about Susan." My mother began to say, *"Oh. Oh. Oh."*
>
> That moment is one of the hardest in my life to look straight at in memory.

She came to the door when we knocked and swept me into her arms before I could say anything. Then she sent my daughters upstairs to join the others, took me into her apartment, and sat me down on the couch. I waited for her to ask me how her daughter had died, but instead she said, "So how are you, Gordon? You've certainly had a hell of a time, haven't you?"

When we'd left to begin our sail she hadn't yet moved into the apartment and was full of reservations about it.

Susan and the others worried she'd go off on her own, in spite of advancing age and perilous finances. Now I could see that the place was cozy and light yet uncompromisingly Victorian. The floors and trim were oak, the ceilings were lofty, and the fireplace was marble. Her stiff Boston furniture seemed at home. The back windows looked out onto a nice yard; the front ones looked out onto respectable Hancock Street. I started to cry.

It felt so good that I kept on and on. We were sitting beside each other on the couch; she put her hand on my forearm. The grandfather clock ticked, then chimed a quarter past six. "It's just that she would have been so relieved to see this place, and you in it," I heard myself say. "You know. How it all turned out."

Her hand tightened. "Well. Thank you for telling me that, Gordon. I have wondered occasionally, you know. If she cared."

"For the best." I nodded. "For the best."

She took her hand away, stood up with a sigh, and walked in stocking feet into the kitchen for the teakettle. Then she poured three cups, and we sat there drinking it as if Susan were with us, looking out the window at the gas lights on Hancock Street and the shadows of the passersby.

Susan's brothers and sister and many of her ten nieces and nephews have the long narrow Atkinson nose, the thin straight lips, the small mouth, the deep-set gray eyes. Seeing them gathered in the living room upstairs was like looking at an artist's variations on her own face.

During the bitter round of hugs, handshakes, and hellos I didn't see her younger sister, Mary, right away; she was in the kitchen. When she came into the room, I clung to her for a long time, taking misplaced comfort in the fact that her body felt like Susan's, and remembering her light, girlish voice when I'd called from Honolulu. "Oh, Gordon, were you having fun? I want to know everything— what you both were wearing, what you were talking about, what you were reading. Were the two of you having the time of your lives?"

Ned stayed in the kitchen. But the others gathered around, and her middle brother, Stephen, the most garrulous and outgoing, began gently and tactfully to ask me questions—as if he understood my desperate need to confess.

I'd brought with me a computer printout of the typhoon's path that sympathetic weather people at the missile base on Kwajalein had made available, clearly showing the storm's unreported change of course that took the eye directly over Wotho atoll.

It was like evidence in a trial that had already been lost. After I'd passed the printout around and was answering Stephen's questions, I imagined I could see the family slowly begin to experience Susan's absence as something horribly permanent instead of just a voice with bad news at the other end of a long-distance phone line. There were no stiff upper lips; the Atkinsons were on familiar terms with emotion. And they showed me mercy.

* * *

"What an amazing family," my daughter Julie said on the drive home. "They were all so . . ."

"Real," Diana said.

It was a soggy word from her Deadhead days, but it sank deep into my mind because since the storm everything for me had been *unreal*. The Atkinson family had taken me in and heard my limp confession with a graciousness and compassion that I couldn't comprehend, couldn't accept.

There was only one person besides me who knew what really had happened, and she was no longer in the world. *Oh, oh, oh, oh,* was the last thing I'd heard her say, and the desperation of it hadn't penetrated. I'd never know what she thought after I failed to hold her up and left her alone in that terrible darkness. Whether she hated me as much as I hated myself, as much as my sister hated me, or the wife of my journalist friend did, and probably the Atkinsons did or would, after they'd had time to think about it. There was not the slightest chance that Ashley and Page could feel any differently about me.

It doesn't get any more real than this, I thought vaguely, trying to live up at last to Susan's sharp-edged awareness that actions have consequences. I only realized later that Susan dying and her grieving family might not have been thinking much about me at all.

Fathers and Daughters

A few days later, Diana drove me to the farm in upstate New York to get my car, clothes, and papers. She was an expert driver after many miles on tour with the Grateful Dead, and I had total confidence in her even on the icy roads. She was thoughtfully playing Bob Dylan instead of Jerry Garcia—"Don't think twice, it's all right."

Not long after crossing the state line out of Massachusetts, I asked her why Holly had been in tears as we prepared to leave, apologizing for something I didn't understand.

"Well," Diana said. "She just lost it when she first heard about Susan. It was like she was back when you guys were splitting up, and all that."

All that.

"She never got over it," Diana said. "It's been bothering her all this time, underneath. And then suddenly she was totally into it again. Crying but angry. Like she was mortified. I started to see things very differently."

"Wow . . . like, what things?" Why, when I was with her, did I talk like an old-time hippie?

"I began to see how she'd influenced me over the years," Diana said, speaking more concisely than I'd ever heard her. "How her resentments and problems had been transmitted to me."

She guided the car deftly around a sharp bend. I felt my head spin.

"I started to see you in a new light," she said. "My own view, not just a version of my mother's."

That my daughters loved me as much as they did was only now beginning to make itself plain to me. Susan was right—I had taken them for granted as small children, in the same way my parents had taken me for granted. "Kids will love you no matter what," I'd always claimed. "They don't have any choice." This was before I left Holly and realized there were some things you could do to make your children stop loving you.

Diana took the breakup hardest. As soon as she'd
graduated from high school, she split for California and
became a full-time Deadhead, worshiping the same band
her mother and I had grooved on twenty years before. She
seemed to be relentlessly cramming my own music down
my throat.

When Diana passed through with a gaggle of friends
on the trail of the next show (Susan and I had a house in
Jersey City Heights not far from the Meadowlands), I asked
a guy they called Zippy about the Deadhead phenomenon.
"It's like it's one big family," he said, staring at me. "Yeah.
They're our family, man."

I'd bailed on my family. And Uncle Jerry had stayed
the course.

Our big blowup occurred when she showed up five
and a half months pregnant with my grandson, Avery, no
male partner in sight. Between shows, she'd been attend-
ing some off-the-wall college in San Francisco. Her mother
was still indulging her, now from my alimony checks. She
was macrobiotic and, except for her belly, as thin as a stick.

While we discussed her future, Diana perched clum-
sily on the edge of a chair, soaking an infected finger in
saline solution. The iron casserole containing it rested on
what was left of her lap.

The discussion turned financial, a topic programmed
for disaster. There was more than money involved—
"Money is love between you two," Susan always said—

and even in the best of times I could never seem to give Diana enough of either. Her face twisted into the grimace of hate I'd become familiar with since I'd left her mother. "I'd like to throw this water right in your face."

Suddenly I lost it—red red rage. I leaned forward and grabbed the heavy little pot out of her hand. "I'll save you the trouble."

With all my strength I swung the pot in a short upward arc toward my face, not allowing for its weight and the long follow-through. The lip crashed into the bridge of my nose, which immediately went numb.

I threw the pot to the floor, and it bounced into the wall, leaving a dent. Then I just sat there, blinded by the pain, dripping salty water and feeling a thicker warm wetness running out of my nose. I heard my daughter screaming as if from a long way off and thanked God I'd been able to turn the violence on myself.

I felt my way out of the office, down the hall, and into our bedroom. Sitting on the bed, shrouded in a fog of pain, I heard the faint screams dwindle and then the brisk noise of Susan bundling Diana out the door and into a taxi. I was thinking, *I hope my nose is splattered.*

"Who's going to take care of you now?" someone asked me at the reception after Susan's memorial service. It was an endearingly tousle-haired young woman, a friend of Susan's sister, Mary. I'd finally bought new glasses and could see people clearly if I had to. Her expression was appropriately solemn and unreadable.

It was a terrifying question. I looked around helplessly and saw Diana standing about ten feet away, watching us. She'd heard. And her expression, I realized with amazement, was full of love.

What price love? Susan herself would never have asked that particular question. Never in a million years.

Now, up at the farm, after Diana had gone to bed in the guest room on the ground floor, I took Susan's old green leather suitcase of memorabilia from the closet in our upstairs bedroom and carried it to the library next door. The suitcase had metal clasps that drummed open when I slid the two buttons sideways. A faint sun-and-sand fragrance drifted from a half-used tube of Bain de Soleil. Nestled in the ivory silk interior were our love letters (Xeroxes of hers), photographs of us in flagrante, a copy of *Sue Barton, Student Nurse,* a longhand manuscript of my first short story, an empty change purse, a pair of sunglasses, a set of keys (to what?), and a cigar box with one Monte Cristo Cuban cigar, a humidifier, and a note. *Sweetheart, I trust you to save this cigar. It's my last one. With all my heart, Gordon.*

Her diaries were there in three notebooks—a large bound one, two smaller paperback ones—and a few folders of loose pages. I began at the beginning, reading guiltily, skimming the pages as fast as I could, not snooping (I told myself) so much as looking for the answer. I was hoping that by some miracle it might pop out at me, even if I wasn't sure about the question.

Spurring me on in my invasion was a vision of Ashley's tight, deathly pale face, as clear as if I'd been sitting opposite her again in the New York restaurant before our goodbye dinner: "Over my dead body you're going to go off and leave her alone. If you don't promise, I'll tie her to my bed so she stays with me."

When she'd said that I'd been floored, unable to deal with its power and certainty. For the last three years I'd kept it down. Now suddenly it was here on the table, and I was terrified of what I might find in Susan's diaries to explain it.

Minutes or hours later, I turned the last page in the last notebook and looked around the room—at the bookshelves, idly picking out old familiar titles; at the photographs of my great-grandfather, grandfather, and uncles in their British regimental uniforms; at the black December windows. Hanging on a nail above one of them was an inheritance from my father, a British Webley .45-caliber officer's revolver.

I stared at the revolver, sensing it was somehow related to what I'd read. I went over and took it down, feeling its weight, the roughness of its checkered walnut grip. I pressed the two catches on either side of the frame, broke it open, checked the empty cylinder, and snapped it closed again. I pulled back the hammer until it clicked into the cocked position.

In Graham Greene's autobiography, I'd read how as a boy he used to play Russian roulette. The first few times, he said, the snap of the hammer made the world fresh, new,

and crystal clear. It occurred to me that that kind of clarity—I remembered the compressed, brilliant moment one
hundred feet down off the Lyford Cay drop-off—was necessary to understand what the answer might be.

There was a box of cartridges in the desk drawer. I took
one out, broke the pistol open again and inserted the cartridge, closed the pistol, spun the cylinder, and laid the piece
down on the red leather desktop. I couldn't lose, because
I'd already won. Fate had already had its shot at me.

I knew I couldn't lose, but what about my daughter?
The trigger is pulled, the shot is fired. Actions have consequences. As clearly as if I were watching it on film, I saw
Diana sit up terrified in the room downstairs, turn on the
light, climb out of bed, and start up the stairs to the library.

As quick as I could, I took the cartridge out of the
cylinder, put it back in the box, put both the revolver and
the box in the desk drawer and closed it. The windows
were lightening.

It was dawn. The door swung open, as I knew it
would. Diana was standing there.

"Have you been up all night?"

"I might have napped a few times. I think I did."

"Are you okay?"

"I think so. Yeah. How did you sleep?"

"The coyotes kept me awake for a while. I saw your
light was on, and I heard you come in here."

"You did?"

"I wondered whether to get up. I didn't know. I
thought. . . ." She was crying. I made a little movement

with my hands and she was kneeling beside the couch, her head on my chest. My arms were around her. We were crying together for the first time I could remember.

"Can you sleep now," she asked finally. "Or do you want some breakfast?"

Easter Sunday

Susan's writing is stylishly informal, sometimes profane, sometimes bitchy, sometimes humorous, but very clear, very pointed. After leaving nursing to write full-time on the occasion of our Mexican sojourn, she produced three novels, many short stories, photo essays, humorous card captions, two self-illustrated children's books, and two cartoon books on marital discord, *It's All His Fault* and *It's All Her Fault*. In a large, forward-slanting, no-nonsense hand she makes entries in her diary when she's confused or angry. She writes long, thoughtful letters to her friends and family, telling them about our travels or dissecting personal issues. She writes bad-tempered letters of complaint and doesn't send them. She keeps date books of each year, telling what happened when. She's a creature of record, a compulsive scribbler. She has trouble with form.

I'm rereading *Taking Off,* her young-adult novel about the disastrous interlude with her daughters in Todos Santos, Baja California. It's narrated by a character based on Page.

When something major is about to happen, something that will change your whole life, there should be advance notice. An alarm would help, and sirens; then a voice over a loudspeaker: *Watch out! After this moment you will not be the same person.* Of course, you never do get any warning. The night we decided to take off and live in Mexico for a year is a perfect example.

Halfway through the year, both daughters leave Mexico to go live with their father. At the end of the manuscript, on their way to the airport, Page's character asks her mother when she's coming back herself.

"I don't know."

"What are you *saying?*" An electric jolt of fear ran through me.

"A year, I'm staying a year. I feel comfortable with that since you'll be with your father. Then I'll return

to the States. Physically, anyway. In spirit . . . well, once
you take this kind of a step I don't think you ever really
come back."

No wonder Susan's daughters left. After all, they were
urban American teenagers and Todos Santos was a little
Mexican village. But as important as change and adventure were to Susan, I know she gladly would have gone
back with them if it hadn't been for one thing. Me. I
wouldn't have come.

I believe she chose me over them. It would be easier
if I'm wrong. But if she did choose me, she kept the secret
even from herself.

Then the mother says wistfully:

"When we were taking off on this pioneer voyage, if
I'd known how it would end . . . "

Would Susan have chosen me anyway? "You have to
act fast when you make a decision," she would have an
swered, with one of those full-on smiles. "It could be wrong."

Actually, though, the trip to Mexico changed Page
more than any of us. After we'd been there a few months
she ditched the Coke-bottle bifocals she'd had to wear since
age seven to correct a wandering eye. She's never worn
them since, confounding ophthalmologists all along the
northeastern seaboard.

I remember how she looked the first morning without her glasses (she and Ashley were dressed in the pink

Mexican school uniforms they hated)—absolutely confident. "Nobody else around here wears geeky bifocals, so I'm not going to either. You know what they call me? *Ocho ojos.* Eight-eyes, Mom. I'm sick of being a pampered little *gringa.*"

We all laughed and I thought, It'll never work, but I admire her spirit.

I'd always admired Page's spirit, always been a little scared of her dark, underdog intensity. I remembered her face on the north rim of the Grand Canyon during an innocuous debate about where to drop our deliquescing Halloween pumpkin so it would have the longest fall into the abyss. "*I hate you! I wish you were dead!*" she screamed at me. The thick lenses magnified her passion.

Once her glasses were shed, the change was miraculous and seemingly effortless. She became a different person, a dark-eyed smoldering Latin beauty. Soon she had an attentive Mexican boyfriend and, in due course, her first kiss.

On Easter Sunday four months after the storm, I found a letter from Page in my mailbox in Berkeley, California, where I'd rented an apartment and had started trying to write. Of course there's no delivery on Easter Sunday. Maybe it had arrived the day before, but how could I have overlooked it? Don't ask me why I happened to look in my mailbox on Easter Sunday, either.

I spend time these days trying to convince
myself that my future can still be good. It's hard,

though. It's a matter of completely changing my visions of the future, but still having them be positive. I think of getting married—I always imagined you and Mom standing in the receiving line—Mom dressed in a stylish little number, looking fabulous. Now she won't be there, and now I try to think about my wedding w/out her there.

I mean, of course, she'll *be* there, and I will include her in the ceremony in a spiritual way—but she won't be there smiling, looking 35, crying, laughing, dancing w/you, her neck craning back looking at you on her tippie toes. And although it sucks I keep my thoughts on the future. I am trying to convince myself that it will still be okay. It will *never* be the same; it will be vastly different, but could still be good. I hope I am right.

I stood there holding the letter and listening to the church bells all over town. Since the storm I'd been like a sleepwalker, moving through a featureless landscape. No beam of light from the outside penetrated. I just reacted to stimuli. No hope. No despair. In my writing, I could describe things and feelings before the storm reasonably well, but after it nothing came but a starkly factual outline.

Standing in the warm April sunshine of Berkeley, I felt something struggle on the other side of the shroud to get through, some feeling or perception that hadn't been forced on me simply by what had been happening. It turned out to be the first feeble gleam of understanding that for me, as well as Page, everything was going to be different from now on, that when I felt Susan's hair slip away from me underwater it was the end of my life too, as I knew it. Page had hope, and she'd done her best to tell me, but she hadn't made the choices that either led or didn't lead to where we are now.

I didn't feel there was much hope for me. Still, the fact that Page had some was more important than anything else since the storm.

A HEART
IN PORT

⚡ ⚡ ⚡

Who I Am

Ashley and Page both made down payments on houses last year with money they'd inherited from Susan, and not long afterward they both got married. Their husbands are alike: strong and silent, down-to-earth. Both daughters began with fund-raising jobs at conservative institutions (their father's influence)—Ashley at the American Enterprise Institute in Washington, Page at the Newport Art Museum—but now work for liberal ones—the *New Republic* and Save the Bay. Susan would be proud, though so far neither has produced any of the grandchildren she'd dreamed of playing with in her dotage.

Ironically, given our disastrous time there, Mexico keeps us in touch. Even after moving back east, Susan had insisted we buy a share of an old abandoned house in Todos Santos so we'd always have a place. Every year before she died we gathered there for the Christmas–New Year's holidays. We still do.

On the New Year's Eve after the storm we drank champagne on the dunes where she'd wanted her ashes spread and on New Year's Day built a memorial in the back yard in the seedy but eloquent style of the Mexican roadside death markers she'd loved. Whale ribs and vertebrae, dolphin skulls she'd collected, a wrought-iron cross we'd found in the shed, a yellow concrete *casita* with wooden doors for candles and relics, and a ceramic painted tile with a sunset and a whale and the words:

SUSAN ATKINSON

1942–1992

Que siga la fiesta!

Que siga la fiesta—let the party continue—was her favorite Mexican expression. Another we both loved was *Si Dios quiere*—if God wishes. Whenever Mexicans announce plans, especially plans involving risk, they end with *Si Dios quiere*. Mankind is not in control.

The idea is more than religion; it's one of the two great ways of looking at the world. Some people believe the world runs according to rational plan; others believe in something outside that. We called it chance and welcomed its challenge. We both loved Mexico. *Si Dios quiere* confirmed what we already knew in our hearts.

Once you take this kind of a step I don't think you ever really come back, Susan had written. Well, she never did come back. There's no memorial to her in the United States, though she would have loved the headline on her two-column obituary in the *Boston Globe*. I hope mine is halfway as good.

SUSAN ATKINSON, 49,
AUTHOR AND ADVENTURER
CAUGHT IN TYPHOON

I didn't come back either. Someone who looks like me and has my name came back. Like Pip, in *Moby-Dick*, I'm not really here anymore. I'm at Wotho atoll with her, planning our next leg.

What kind of a step had we taken, exactly? All I can say for sure is that before the storm we were happier than we'd ever been before. If there was any pattern in our lives, it was the one that led us to go adventuring, to pursue what we knew was the way the world worked, to put ourselves firmly and without question in the hands of chance.

We went where it led us, and in the end it produced the defining moment of our lives.

A couple of years after the storm, I came across a disturbing book, *Broken Vessels,* by André Dubus. He describes

stopping late one summer night on I-93 north of Boston
to help with a breakdown. Two young Latins, brother and
sister, are standing with their car in the middle of the highway. Dubus parks his own car as far onto the median strip
as the guardrail allows and walks over to see what he can do.
The three of them are standing there next to the broken-
down car as the headlights of a third car approach. At the
last moment Dubus realizes the approaching car is swerving toward them.

His reflex at that moment is to pull the woman out of
the way, not to jump out of the way himself. The woman
is saved, but the car hits Dubus full on, mangling his legs.
(It also hits the woman's brother, who later dies.) The rest
of the book describes how Dubus copes first with the pain
of his ruined legs and then with being in a wheelchair for
the rest of his life. His crippling is bearable largely because
he knows that during the moment of truth he did the right
thing. Not because of any conscious decision, but because
that's who he was. So he found out.

You never know who you really are until the moment comes.

There were many decisions that led or did not lead to
our own moment, depending on which view of the world
you have. We made most of them together, but there was
never any real doubt as to who the captain was. Susan wanted
it that way. It was part of her fantasy, part of mine too.

Some of the decisions were not errors, such as the
decision to sail to the Marshall Islands in November, when

there was still a chance of typhoons in the western North Pacific. We could have erred on the side of caution and started the voyage a month later, but such was not our nature. We had places to go and things to do, and we knew we were lucky.

Our decision to stay at Wotho and wait for the storm to pass instead of sailing away was a reasonable one too. Who knew what the odds were of Gay swerving to make a direct hit on us? They were small enough, anyway, that to have it happen one would have to be very unlucky—or to be somehow targeted. Once it did happen, though, the boat was doomed.

But . . . why didn't I listen to the advice of the Wotho Islanders and my own senses and swim us ashore after the spring line broke and it should have been obvious that the typhoon was not passing us by? Why didn't I check out the life jackets more thoroughly, and have a life jacket drill? Why did I have only inflatable life jackets instead of Coast Guard–approved foam-filled ones aboard my boat? Why didn't I get our wet suits out of the forepeak earlier? *Why was she on the boat that night at all?*

Because.

Either by accident or design, my moment was upon me. I could feel Susan's hair with my fingertips as she drifted down and away. My choice was to let go of my half-inflated life jacket and try to swim down after her—or not.

She would have been groggy with swallowed water. If I'd found her I would have had to get her back to the surface and keep her head up so she could breathe. Both life jackets would have been gone so I'd have had no support other than my own kicking. Holding her up in the breaking waves would have exhausted me fast.

Still, land might have been a few seconds away, for all I knew. If we'd been lucky, there was a chance I could have gotten her ashore and gotten the water out of her—resuscitated her.

If we'd been lucky.

With hindsight, I can see how the sequence of events leading up to this moment had changed my feeling about luck. We had been lucky, incredibly lucky, for most of our lives, but now our luck had run out. One thing after another failed us, and as they did, that passive feeling—like Dr. Livingston's inert acceptance of a lion's mauling in Africa—had grown stronger.

Land was nowhere around. How could it be? I was sure we were being sucked out into the open ocean through a channel in the reef. The time for heroism seemed long gone.

It wasn't, of course. In hindsight, if I'd found her I could have died with her in my arms, trying to save her until the last minute. But hindsight wasn't yet available. I chose to live as long as possible.

Dreams

It's August, more than two and a half years after the storm. I'm trying to write about it in my office in the garage of our place in upstate New York. It's a rainy Saturday. Mist hangs over the tops of the hills, the eaves drip slowly, and a flock of half-grown wild turkeys forage with their mother in the top corner of the hayfield. Wet weather always brings them out.

This summer is the first time I've dared to come back for longer than a weekend. The retired couple I've rented to have agreed to swap residences for two months; they're in my apartment in New York City.

Above the desk in my office is a birthday present from Susan: a Victorian gilt oval frame filled with hundreds of glass eyes. They're from a taxidermy mail-order house: little blue ones with slit pupils, big brown ones with oblong pupils, smaller brown ones with ovoid pupils, big yellow ones, small red ones, small yellow ones. The eyes are pasted in patterns on a black background in the oval frame. Ringing the animal eyes and interspersed with them are dolls' eyes that open and close if moved and have thick eyelashes. The title of the piece is "Here's Looking at You."

On another wall of the office is a framed chart of the *Lord Jim*'s maiden voyage down the Mosquito Coast of Central America. Our route is etched in little black arrows, and our various ports of call have been inscribed in black-letter. A beautifully detailed old-fashioned compass rose takes up the ocean space between Cuba and the Misteriosa Bank, and the *Lord Jim* herself, rendered in ink with all sails set, is exiting the Gulf of Mexico close-hauled—another birthday present. And another, in the living room—a mahogany woodcut of the *Lord Jim*, seen through the foliage of a jungly coast; it was taken from the dust cover of *Fever Coast Log*.

The house is full of Susan's gifts, around any corner, in all kinds of unexpected places. A papier-mâché Canada goose, in honor of all my fruitless wild-goose chases. A neon sign reading SURF'S UP. A block of granite inscribed with my name, the date I bought the house, and the words *Hic Domus Est*.

A truck bug shield emblazoned with *Stanley Creek Farm Duck-mobile*. An oil painting commissioned from her ex-sister-in-law of me surfing an overhead wave in Baja California.

In the beginning, I thought about putting them all in storage, but it would have been easier to shut myself away. Still, I went out of my way to avoid them, making detours, staying out of certain rooms. Then, piece by piece, I began to need them. Finally, I moved "Here's Looking at You" from the living room to my office, and now I stare back at it when my mind goes blank.

She feels close . . . especially when I climb up through the hayfields and hedgerows to the top of the hill behind the house, where you can get a 360-degree view of the countryside and there's less air separating you from heaven. It was always her favorite place, and every time I go up I believe that at last I'll hear her voice. I can imagine it saying, a touch irritably, "So what took you so long? I've been waiting here forever—not that I mind that much." But so far, nothing but the sound of the wind in the grass and sometimes my own voice carrying on my half of the conversation.

I've had very few dreams since the storm, and the ones I remember are fragmentary, disconnected images and vignettes. For two and a half years, Susan has been absent from me, though she appears regularly in dreams to everybody else who knew her.

A few days ago I drove down to Boston to say goodbye to Susan's mother. Her cancer, which she'd fought off for seven years, had flared up. She was in a partial coma and not expected to live through the week. The only thing she said to me in the hours I sat beside her hospital bed was in answer to my question about her dreams. Had she been having any interesting ones? (I didn't say the name I wanted to hear.) Her eyes flew open. "Not particularly," she said distinctly, looking at something in the far distance. I thought about inventing one of my own with Susan in it but decided not to. In a few minutes her eyes closed again, and they were closed when I left. She died a few days later.

Back at the farm, when I finally fall asleep I dream there is a mirror in the corner of my vision. Something is reflected in it. When I turn to look, I see the image of Susan looking back matter-of-factly. She has no expression on her face. The mirror cuts off the bottom half of her body, but it looks as if she's wearing a black sleeveless dress. The image is so clear it makes me jump.

She is there but not there. Clear, but only reflected. Silent and expressionless.

Up at the Farm

September 1995. I've just listed the farm for sale, and I walk out the half-mile two-track road to the mailbox feeling light on my feet. The rain has stopped, but it's still too misty to see into the Hudson River Valley below, much too misty to see the Adirondacks on the other side. Some young maples are beginning to yellow, the color fluorescent in the mist like the house. Susan got sick of white that last summer, and now the house is brilliant canary. The muddy road shows fresh tracks of turkey, deer, rabbit, coyote. In the misty pasture looms a black-and-white Holstein heifer. She was terrified of cows.

There's one letter in the mailbox. It happens to be from Page. I'm not surprised. I've been thinking about her, and since the storm I involuntarily search for reasons why things happen the way they do. For example, when I looked in the little *casita* of Susan's memorial last New Year's I discovered her favorite book of Patricia Highsmith's Ripley stories I'd been wanting to reread but had given up for lost. And after we'd toasted her with champagne that New Year's after the storm, we'd found an empty glass on top of the highest dune where we'd put her full one. Just chance?

I fold the letter, put it in my pocket, and walk back down the two-track. The trees drip. Robins sound their echoing limpid rain song. Suddenly—*blapppp*—a ruffed grouse explodes from a wild apple tree, hurtling across the road and down into the birches near the swamp. I take it as another sign. Susan and I hunted grouse every fall, rarely shooting them but always loving that first blast.

Past the wild roses, slogging up the muddy hay-wagon track to the top of the hill behind the house. Out of breath, blood lagging, I reach the top of the first field and turn as always to see the house and its outbuildings nestled at the bottom and the Hebron hills rolling away.

Across the old abandoned road into the upper field— God's country, as the farmer who works it says—with the mist breaking up into light-shot canyons and raindrops sitting intact on alfalfa leaves, Queen Anne's lace, cornflowers, goldenrod, poppies, dandelions, black-eyed Susans (she loves me, she loves me not).

It has been said that out of every bad situation something positive will come. For me I guess it is my absolute exuberance for everything in life. Mom's death clearly points out the need to really live, to not plan for things that will happen later at the expense of things that are happening right now. My friend Heidi worries about me now. She feels I am reckless and that my enthusiasm is exhausting. Well, I think she has just not gotten used to the way I look at things now and the way I do things. I'm not reckless; I'm adventurous. I'm not overly enthusiastic; I'm interested. I guess the difference in my life now is that I understand I have to make my choices: enjoy the good choices, learn from the bad. It's weird—for the first time in my life I am self-aware. I am aware that my happiness, my career, my marriage, my friendships are all up to me. And now in my life, I really *want* things. I live my life aware at every moment that I am hoping I am impressing Mom, trying to live up to her standards, many of which I didn't live up to when she was alive. Now, even though she is gone she is still my motivating factor, my cheerleader. I wouldn't want it any other way. I think often of her sense of fairness; her limitless love and forgiveness for her friends and family; her love of reading and writing; the way she jiggled when she was telling a joke she thought was really funny; her obvious enjoyment of being in the kitchen in Hebron or Mexico cooking, laughing, making dinner; her exuberance; her sensitivity that allowed her to notice and appreciate qualities in others that most people wouldn't know existed.

I miss Mom an incredible amount. Do you? Do you still feel her influencing you, who you are, what you do? Do you wonder what she might say about a story you've written or a trip you've been on? I'm just curious.

If I'm ever going to hear her voice, it will be now. I wait and wait, and finally start back down. I realize I've already heard it.

Where Are
We Going?

I've taken up flying again. There's a wonderful airport near
the farm, a single bumpy asphalt strip (with an incidental
graveyard at each end) and dusty hangars filled with fabric-
covered single-engined tail-draggers from the forties and
fifties. Spare parts are hoarded away in different piles. The
planes are flown every day by a fanatic group of regulars
who keep them in perfect condition. The pilots fly late,
after the chores have been done.

I get a late start myself one evening, in the Piper J-3.
I have an hour of light left, and the sun is due to set even

sooner. It's one of the sweetest evenings of the year—warm, clear, still, the tail end of a high-pressure system. The little airport drowses in the quiet, the late-summer crickets in the grass seem louder than the few planes that are up. The stray dogs and cats adopted by the airport owner's wife lounge on the warm asphalt with their ears pricked, listening to the last sound of summer before it slips away.

The air, as I take off, is smooth as the surface of Lake St. Catherine, off to the east, where a lone speedboat and waterskier divide it into two silver mirrors. Golden sunset ground mist is beginning to gather in the deepest hollows.

I'm wearing earphones. Through them, over some light static, I hear, or think I hear, a familiar voice. *Where are we going?*

At the moment we're climbing at 70 knots under full power, the light plane's best rate of climb. We are at 1,000 feet on a heading of 160 degrees, just over the high school football field where the Golden Horde is finishing up a preseason practice. We're beginning a slow turn to the west, into the setting sun, holding the angle of climb and the power on full and keeping the airspeed at 70 knots.

At 2,000 feet, we can see over the Hebron hills into the Hudson River Valley, the river catching the light in the distance, and the two high-rise buildings in Glens Falls outlined in magenta every bit as vivid as buttes in the Grand Canyon. We roll out of the gentle turn at 270 degrees, due west, and keep climbing. *All right!* I hear over the earphones. Or is it me?

My personal ceiling is 5,000 feet. Around here, there's no need to go higher; the highest point is Mount Equinox, near Manchester, Vermont, only 3,816. Still, when we get there, the sound of the 90-hp Continental engine is steady, and the oil temperature and pressure gauges register normal. The sun is only a few inches from the top of the Adirondack range in front of us, and the little lakes scattered through it are glittering silver. We keep on climbing.

At this rate of climb we're fighting a slightly losing battle. The sun is still going down, though only about half as fast. At 8,000 feet, we are still well in the light, but the shadows are beginning to creep eastward from the Adirondacks, and the thin clouds over and ahead of us are blazing salmon. It's cooler up here, and we've risen above a visible thermocline into even clearer air.

Gradually, the landscape purples and fades, even as the light around us seems to grow. At 10,000 feet we are held up by the light, heading into it as if into a strong current.

Acknowledgments

This book began as pure therapy. Making the transition to a publishable work from highly personal woolgatherings, love-ramblings, euphoria, hallucinations, should-have-dones, excuses, and mea culpas, through many many drafts and years, would never have been possible without the encouragement and help of a select corps of friendly readers who never begrudged their time and talent. Surely a more diverse group would be hard to imagine—I'd love to gather them all together for a little while in the same room, but that could never happen. In chronological order of their contributions, they are: Jonathan Penner, Thomas Powers, Darcie Gannon, Betty Green, Marissa Bridge, Katharine Ogden, and Julia Chaplin. My agent Tina Bennett's forceful enthusiasm, and my editor Elisabeth Schmitz's wonderfully sensitive and painstaking refinements were beyond anything I could have hoped for.

To Susan's family and friends, who have viewed this work with understandably mixed feelings, all I can say is that I did the best I could. This may ring hollow, coming from someone whose best wasn't good enough. I know that better than I know anything. Still, I had to try.

THE CRUISE OF THE LORD JIM

1989-1992

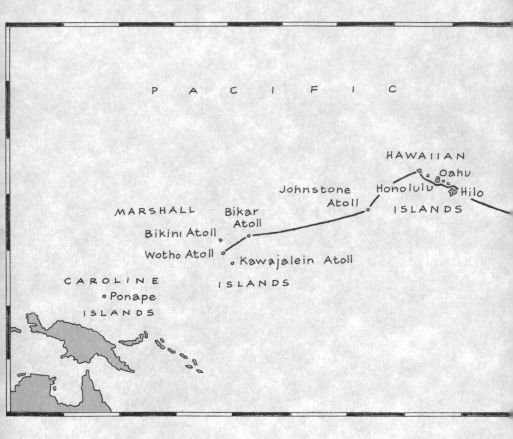